The Dialectic of
World Politics

About the Author

Silviu Brucan is a professor of international relations at the University of Bucharest, where he received a Ph.D. in philosophy.

A long-time activist in the political arena, he was a participant in the anti-Fascist underground movement in Romania during World War II. From 1956-1959 he served as Romania's Ambassador to the United States, followed by three years as Romania's Ambassador to the United Nations.

Professor Brucan is the author of numerous books and articles on international relations.

The Dialectic of World Politics

Silviu Brucan

THE FREE PRESS
A Division of Macmillan Publishing Co., Inc.
NEW YORK

Collier Macmillan Publishers
LONDON

The Free Press
A Division of Macmillan Publishing Co., Inc.
866 Third Avenue, New York, N.Y. 10022

Collier Macmillan Canada, Ltd.

Library of Congress Catalog Card Number: 77-85349

Printed in the United States of America

printing number

1 2 3 4 5 6 7 8 9 10

Library of Congress Cataloging in Publication Data

Brucan, Silviu
    Marxist theory of international relations.

    Includes bibliographical references and index.
    1. Communism. 2. Socialism. 3. International relations. I. Title.
HX550.I5B78 1978   335.43'8'327   77-85349
ISBN 0-02-904680-7

Contents

Preface

THE GENERATION THAT SURVIVED World War II lived for almost fifteen years with the image of a world divided along ideological lines. Two opposite and hostile camps, capitalism and socialism, West and East, each one tightly lined up behind its leading power, the United States and the Soviet Union, were cleft by an antagonism so bitter that a showdown seemed inevitable.

At the end of the 1950s, rather suddenly, this straight and clear-cut picture painted in the classic academic manner with definite boundaries and precise contours turned into a dizzy nonfigurative painting in which the boundaries were blurred, while lines intersected, crosscut and overlapped each other. It all began with Charles de Gaulle's rejection of "American hegemony" in the West and the harsh Sino-Soviet polemics in the East; it went on with the jointly drafted Soviet-American test-ban and nonproliferation treaties, followed by the "heretic" visit of President Nixon to Peking, the invasion of Czechoslovakia by the "brotherly armies," the bizarre constellation in both the Indo-Pakistani war of 1971 and the war in Angola of 1976, where the U.S. and China found themselves on one side of the fence while the U.S.S.R. stood firmly on the other. Last but not least, a number of kingdoms, sheikdoms and emirates of the Persian Gulf, surviving from other ages, carried out an oil embargo that shook some of the rich and arrogant power centers to their very foundations.

Those who had become used to the idea of the two camps now stand baffled and perplexed before this "big news." What happened to this world of ours?

Lenin once spoke of a paradox or "dialectical puzzle" as he referred to the need of preserving, in the early stage of socialist construction, "not only the bourgeois right but even the bourgeois state—without the bourgeoisie." Apparently, this should now be extended to international politics, for we live in a world in which the socialist nations must adapt themselves to the patterns of behavior prevailing in the international system.

Karl Marx repeatedly warned against a purely linear view of history unfolding in accordance with a sort of cumulative chronology in which one social formation (feudalism or capitalism) suceeds and supersedes the next to produce the successor that will surpass it in turn. In fact, history never advances as a linear and straightforward process, but rather in a contradictory way, with sharp turns and detours, advances and setbacks, the new social forces getting their way only ultimately. Indeed, the whole capitalist era has revealed the remanent force of the feudal legacy, and we have witnessed a reactivation of the feudal spell even in the passage to socialism.

However, the *dialectical* component of Marx's philosophy has proved much more difficult to assimilate than the *materialist* one. Whereas the materialist perception is commonsensical and almost consonant with man's natural instincts and primary aims, dialectics is precisely the reverse. Very often it requires us to see both the image of present reality and its possible negation. This is not easy and, as experience shows, poses an almost insuperable obstacle for those in power.

I wrote this book with the principal aim of restoring the balance between the two components of *dialectical materialism*, particularly in the study of world affairs. To this end I endeavor to make up for a fundamental lacuna of Marxism: its almost exclusive focus on one type of social aggregation, namely *classes*, while neglecting the other, that is *ethnicity*.

The conceptual framework of this book is built on the premise that it is the aggregation of men according to these two basic social relationships that conditions their behavior and thinking whenever they act collectively. Although the two intertwine and interact within various types of societies, each has a different historical origin and an evolution of its own. Revolutions that have meant the passing of power from one *class* to another have not altered the characteristics of the ethnic groups involved. The French nation remained French after its 1848 revolution, and so did the Russians, Ukrainians and Georgians after the 1917 October revolution maintain their nationalities.

Looking at the long cycles of human history I discover a certain *dialectical regularity* running through all types of social formations. Starting with the original conflict in ancient times between the centrifugal effect of autonomy within tribes and villages and the centripetal urge for their aggregation into large units, the same dialectical conflict is at work today. National resurgence with its modern version of autonomy called sovereignty clashes with the urge for interdependence, cooperation, and eventually integration.

It is this dialectical regularity that has compounded the class struggle in modern society, thus obtaining a highly sophisticated interplay: on the one hand, nations are torn by inner social conflicts and the contending classes look for support in the international environment; on the other hand, whenever nations are struggling for independence, waging a war, or perceiving a threat from outside, an impulse toward unity among their component classes and social groups permeates the whole community. As one or the other facet expands on a large international scale it may well become predominant in the whole international system. Hence, modern history beginning with the French Revolution has been marked by class conflict alternated by sharp national rivalries. I call this historical interplay the seesaw of class and national motive forces in international politics. For as one comes to prevail, the other goes down, diminishing its impact on a nation's foreign policies.

World War II is a classical example of the priority gained by national motivation and the strategic interests that go with it: The United States and Britain as well as the Soviet Union passed over their class-ideological differences to unite against the common enemy. In occupied countries, too, class conflicts were minimized in the name of national liberation.

After the war, as the revolutionary process extended into Eastern Europe, the United States and other Western powers countered with the containment policy; class conflict and the ideology that goes with it got first priority in world politics. The Cold War was its virulent expression.

With the halting of the revolutionary wave in Europe and the nationalist resurgence of the newly independent states pervading world politics against the background of the nuclear stalemate and primacy of the two superpowers, a new stage opened up at the end of the fifties. The national-strategic motive force again went to the top. This is still the position of the seesaw now and I submit that here lies the explanation of the bizarre partnerships and coalitions that have crosscut ideological lines in the sixties and seventies.

To substantiate this position the book proceeds with a survey of the historical relations between the two essential forms of human aggregation—classes and ethnic communities—and on that basis reaches the conclusion that the contemporary dynamics of these two groups are so different from each other that the researcher must now operate at two levels of analysis— a *national* system and a *world* system—and then study their mutual interaction. Hence two analytical models are offered, one for the study of national foreign policy making, the other for the study of world politics. The explanatory power of both is tested in the analysis of integration, international organizations, and transnational corporations. Their predictive power is applied to the projection of world political developments in the 1980s and of a long-term perspective—the year 2000 and beyond.

In this venture, I start from the assumption that modern technology is a powerful force driving people, things, and processes toward a shrinking world, compelling its subsystems, particularly nation-states, to cooperate more closely in order to regulate the various activities that transcend national borders and eventually to integrate into larger units than the nation-state.

Yet, here again, because of social cleavages inside societies and rivalries among nations the drive of modern technology does not operate as a one-directional sweep, but as a dual and contradictory motion. The effect is a dialectical interplay between the factors that make for division and conflict and those that make for cohesion and integration. The best illustration of this is the vagarious history of the European Economic Community, where moments of elation about political union have been followed by discordant decisions of individual members on monetary policies and imports that have threatened even the basic customs union.

Accordingly, we expect the process of integration to be marked by progress and regression, advances and setbacks, and to proceed in stages, reaching a global dimension only in a very distant future (perhaps the late twenty-first century). It is my assumption that geographical and ecological factors will determine the process to proceed first on a *regional* basis.

Unlike most projections of future worlds, including voguish doomsday predictions, that are long in technological change and short in *social change*, I feel that in the world system changes in one element produce changes in the other elements, and as a result the ensemble undergoes change. Consequently, in the technological cosmos of the next century most if not all sociohistorical categories existing today (classes, nations, states, national powers, etc.) are bound to change and eventually disappear. The fact that they display unusual vigor in contemporary societies may well be attributed to the dialectical phenomenon that makes social categories perish as a result of their own development.

In the meantime, the remaining two decades of this century may go down in history as its most critical and explosive period. For never before have so many social and political contradictions requiring structural changes converged in a world so small and so capable of destroying itself.

Hence the sobering conclusion of this book is that the overriding challenge of the next decades of painful transition may not be the control of population, energy, pollution, or weather, but the control of power.

I am perfectly aware that this book is only an opening statement in the formulation of a global theory of international relations. Such a theory is absolutely essential at a time when the international dimension of change has become decisive.

Acknowledgments

THIS BOOK IS FIRST OF ALL a product of the intellectual climate of Romania and of the growing struggle against dogmatic thinking. Among those who either inspired me through their works or gave me the benefit of their advice and criticism, I owe a special debt to Ion Ceterchi, Valter Roman, and Ovidiu Trasnea (political scientists), Tudorel Postolache and Ilie Serbanescu (economists), Henri Wald and Alexandru Tanase (philosophers), I.V. Galan (novelist), Mihail Botez, Bernard Bereanu and Solomon Marcus (mathematicians), and Cornel Bogdan (diplomat).

I am deeply grateful to the students and professors of the Government Department at Dartmouth, where I tested most of the ideas advanced in this book. The lively discussions and particularly the critical remarks greatly contributed to the clarification of my own thinking and to the strenghtening of my arguments wherever necessary. Here, I must single out Professor Gene Lyons.

Special thanks are due to my wife, Sasha, my daughter, Anca (who drew the research designs), and to all my friends in Bucharest and New York. Anyone who has wrestled with a book like mine written in a foreign language will recognize how important the devotion of friends is in bringing it to an end.

An unwritten rule requires authors to assume full and exclusive responsibility for their book. In my special case such a statement is a must.

1. The Decisive Factor in International Relations?

THE STUDY OF INTERNATIONAL RELATIONS has not always constituted an independent field of inquiry. Both historians and jurists sought to establish this field as a subordinate branch of history and international law, respectively. Indeed, many seventeenth- and eighteenth-century studies attest to this second-class status. Richard Zouche, who in 1650 introduced the notion "intergentes" approached problems of international relations from a juridical standpoint heavily drawing upon Roman law. In the 1870s Albert Sorel and Emile Bourgeois wrote historical works that emphasized diplomatic relations, strategies of kings and maneuvers of royal envoys (official and secret). Both Sorel and Bourgeois recognized the role of national traditions in diplomacy. In this regard they analyzed the impact of geography as well as that of national character on foreign policy (see, for example, Sorel's brilliant *L'Europe et la révolution française).* Foreign policy was then conducted by kings, popes and chancelleries; dynastic, interfeudal and religious considerations prevailed.

The nineteenth century, bringing crucial clarifications and delimitations in all the social sciences, heralded a broader conception of international relations. Though the historical approach was retained, major studies in this field no longer focused exclusively on the diplomatic stratagems of kings and diplomats like Talleyrand, Metternich, and Orlov. Scholars began to explore new facets of reality and to scrutinize causes and issue areas that yielded a better understanding of positions taken by various powers and their rulers.

The whole process of nation formation and centralization of power that accompanied the rise of capitalism required a departure from old modes and frameworks of political thought. This radical shift was magnificently effectuated by the founders of modern

1

political science: Jean Bodin in France, Thomas Hobbes in England, and Niccolò Machiavelli in Italy. They made the concepts of power and state central to political thought, while the study of politics, as Marx put it, was liberated from the tutelage of religion and morality.

Hobbes was the first political thinker to emphasize the role of the state in maintaining peace and order: whereas the state is endowed with supreme power within its own territory, on the international scene the law of the jungle, or what Hobbes called the "state of nature," reigns supreme and "human life is mean, nasty, brutish and short." As the celebrated author of *Leviathan* pointed out: "Hereby it is manifest, that during the time men live without a common power to keep them all in awe, they are in that condition which is called war."[1] This fundamental thesis generated a major current of thought that takes the distinction between *internal politics* and *international politics* as a starting assumption. The Hobbesian proposition therefore must be considered to be the theoretical core of international relations as an autonomous discipline.

Gradually, scholars came to realize that international relations should be viewed as a coherent whole of mutual interactions and connections—economic, political, ideological, juridical, diplomatic, and military—among states and systems of states. The question that remained unanswered was: is there a priority among all these factors? To put it more aggressively, which factor is decisive or determinative? What makes international relations tick?

In his general introduction to *The History of International Relations*,[2] Pierre Renouvin summarized the major approaches to research in this field: the traditional method, which focuses on relations among governments (particularly on statesmen and diplomats), and the new methods, which emphasize the study of the material and spiritual life of societies as relations among peoples. Renouvin showed that some authors view human societies chiefly in terms of their relationship with the geographical environment, the conditions of material existence, the economic structures and their changes, and the character of civilizations; whereas others see the great "historic forces"[3] as sentiments and collective passions related to temperament, traditions, and ways of thinking. To understand international relations, the latter school argued, one must first know the thought process, the spiritual and moral inclinations, and the conception of national interest characteristic of the peoples involved. Renouvin pointed out that historians had thus far avoided making an a priori choice among the different methods but that all assumed that their task was not to isolate single aspects of reality but rather to search everywhere for the elements of an explanation.[4]

While this assumption has the merit of taking into account the complexity of factors operating on the international scene, it is too eclectic. The student who attempts to use it runs the risk of getting lost in the vast labyrinth of international relations. Is there a thread of Ariadne that may guide us through this labyrinth? Let us consider the answers proposed by various schools of thought.

PSYCHOLOGICAL-BEHAVIORIST ANSWER

The psychological (and ultimately behaviorist) school, which dominated until recently the modern science of international relations, offers several methods and research techniques of particular efficiency.[5] The psychosociological approach was born in the 1930s as the study of the attitudes of nations toward war at a time when Hitler's rise to power turned war into a burning issue. The assumption was that on the basis of the study of psychological reactions one could explain and predict the attitudes nations would take in a war. Accordingly, psychological principles derived from studies of human behavior in other settings were applied to international relations, particularly to such phenomena as war, nationalism, and aggression.

In recent years, behaviorism in political science has been denounced as concealing an ideology of "empirical conservatism."[6] Indeed, overemphasis on psychological reactions tends to conceal the profound social and economic sources of conflict, especially class antagonisms and economic inequalities in society, as well as disparities in power or economic development among nations. However, social psychology does play an important part in politics and to ignore or underestimate the psychosocial factor in analyses of social groups or of personalities wielding decisionmaking power would be counterproductive. While Nazi Germany's policy can be explained primarily in terms of socioeconomic and political conditions, international standing, and national goals, a thorough analysis of that period must certainly include the personal role played by Hitler, his character and psychology, and his appeal to the masses. However, the thrust for expansion and domination that prevailed in fascist Germany was grounded in the imperialist structure of a great power, and Hitler's paranoiac behavior acquired political potential only in the context of a political system in which power was entirely concentrated at the top. In other words, psychological reactions and behavior, collective as well as individual, become significant only if they are not dissociated from their original social context.

In focusing upon the human dimension, the psychosociological school developed research methods and techniques particularly fruitful at the micropolitical level. The analysis of *decisionmaking*,[7] for example, is of great importance in the nuclear era, when vital decisions that may involve the survival of mankind are necessarily made by a very few people at the top; surely, their perception of the nature of conflicts, their assessment of their nation and of the potential adversaries, as well as their behavior under stress are of major significance (consider the Cuban missile crisis).

Therefore, we can readily agree with Herbert Kelman that there can be no psychological theory of international relations but only a general theory of international relations "in which psychological factors play a part once the points in the process to which they are applicable have been properly identified."[8]

BIO-ORGANIC AND POWER THEORY

The bio-organic school came into being in the nineteenth century by applying biological laws, particularly Darwin's theories, to relations among nations and races. In his famous work *Der Rassenkampf*, Ludwig Gumplowicz formulated the theory that differentials among races and nations lead to inevitable conflicts among them and that the resulting struggle is so overpowering that it determines not only the inner structure of society but also the character of the individuals who comprise it.

Geopolitics introduced a new, deterministic factor to this school. Rudolf Kjellen, the father of geopolitics, argued that since man is the product of his natural environment, his ideas, motivations, and interests are but the reflection of this environment. Friedrich Ratzel carried this idea to the conclusion that foreign policy is determined by geographic setting. Gustav Ratzenhofer and J. Novikow combined this proposition with Darwin's theory of the survival of the fittest. H. S. Chamberlain, Joseph Arthur de Gobineau, and later on Alfred Rosenberg, the Nazi theoretician, synthesized all these currents in the theory of vital space, *Lebensraum*, claiming that a certain incongruity exists between state borders and the space required by the more "dynamic" nations or races.

Thus, the bio-organic school served as the ideological rationalization of eighteenth- and nineteenth-century imperialist and colonial expansion. It was given fullest expression in Hitler's Germany, which proclaimed Aryan superiority and preached its sacred right to subjugate less dynamic nations in order to achieve world domination.

The racist line of the bio-organic conception has been toned down in contemporary international studies and so have its various imperialist shibboleths such as the "white man's burden," "la mission sacrée," "Manifest Destiny," and "Deutschland über alles." Yet Spencer's organicism identifying the laws of society with those of biology is still propounded by authors who maintain that nations are born, grow old, and die.

A bio-organic notion with a large and strong following today in international studies is Hans Morgenthau's struggle-for-power theory (adapted from Darwin's struggle for life). Morgenthau argues that international politics, like all politics, is necessarily a struggle for power because power is the result of forces inherent in human nature.[9] Again, the root cause of international behavior is traced to biology.

Marxist theory rejects biological reductionism in explaining social phenomena, and criticizes both the application of Darwin's theory to society and Spencer's organicism. Rather, Marxists hold that while society certainly comprises biological processes, it represents a more complex type of material unity qualitatively different from the biological aggregate. In society, biological laws are integrated within the economic and social relations established among people, as well as within the political and ideological conceptions generated by this framework, eventually forming a whole that functions in accordance with social laws that are distinct in many ways from biological principles. Accordingly, men who are biologically strong may well become socially underprivileged and economically poor because of specific societal conditions.

Marxists thus maintain that power should be explained in *social* rather than biological terms; in society, power is an effect rather than a cause, a means rather than an end. Far from being the prime mover in international politics, power is the result of a historical state of affairs defined both by the material conditions of society and by social and national inequalities. Power politics would not and could not exist if nations were equal in size and might.

While Morgenthau's proposition that power is a major factor in both domestic and international politics is valid, his generalization that the struggle for power is a permanent element of all social relations is highly debatable. Hypothetically, if one eliminated the main cause of power, namely, social and national inequality, there would be no reason for domination and struggle against domination; there would be no reason to exercise power. Nor could industrially advanced nations exploit poorer countries if all nations were at the same level of economic and technological development. In the real world, however, nations are great and small, mighty and weak, developed and underdeveloped, rich and poor: as long as such differences exist, power will remain an important factor in international politics.

TECHNOLOGICAL IMPERATIVE

The technological school appeared virtually overnight in the sixties. Modern technology is described by its proponents as an all-powerful Moloch who does and undoes almost everything in society and world politics. "Technological change" has become a catchword in their writings as has "technological imperative."

At one time the thesis that production or technology is ultimately the determining factor in the development of society was dismissed as "Marxist nonsense" or with some similar epithet; professors of international affairs did not want to hear about productive forces having anything to do with their discipline. Indeed, the indexes of leading American textbooks of the 1920s and 1930s included no entries for such items as science, technology, or inventions.[10] Yet anthropologists kept showing that the technology of primitive societies—axe, hoe, and adze; spear, trap, and bow and arrow; and dugouts or canoes and fishing nets—was too simple to allow people to produce more than they could consume and that this fundamental, limiting economic condition determined the character of tribal life. Other anthropologists were documenting how the domestication of animals and the development of agriculture produced a surplus of goods for intertribal exchange and gradually an accumulation of wealth that eventually split primitive societies into classes and generated large-scale, predatory warfare. Emile Durkheim, too, was then demonstrating how the nature of religion and ritual and of law and morality altered with the increasing division and specialization of labor.

It was the production of material goods and the need to exchange them for other goods that impelled and enabled human communities to go outside their narrowly circumscribed territories. And it was the industrial revolution and the tremendous development of productive forces under capitalism that ended the age-old isolation of countries and continents and created the world market. Capturing in one sentence the essence of this process, the British historian G. M. Trevelyan noted that England discovered its "maritime vocation" only after the industrial revolution.

Nevertheless, it took a new scientific revolution, with its tremendous effect on industrial production, to shake up bourgeois sociologists and international relations scholars and make them accept the idea of technology as a determining element in social development. Today, the idea that technology transforms every feature of the environment in which international politics is conducted has gained near unanimous acceptance.

Harold Sprout and Margaret Sprout went as far as drawing up a table entitled "Technological Advance in the Context of International Politics"[11] in which periods of modern history and international events were allegedly determined by inventions brought into general use. As an illustration, Sprout and Sprout established a direct relationship between the major international events in the period 1650–1815 (the European wars, the American Revolution, the French Revolution, the Napoleonic wars, and the Peace of Vienna) and the corresponding inventions (steam engine, mobile "horse artillery," smoothbore musket, primitive rifled small arms, and explosive artillery shells). This is a jump from one extreme to another—outdoing the most inveterate champions of economic materialism! (See pages 11-12 of this volume.)

IDEALIST SCHOOL

The idealist school was inspired by the Enlightenment philosophy of the Marquis de Condorcet, who held forth the promise of a world without war, free of power politics and tyranny, a world guided by rationality and noble ideas: the philosophy of rising capitalism. Idealism depicts an international system rid of conflicts and violence and ruled by principles and law. Woodrow Wilson was a most eloquent spokesman for that school, hailing the League of Nations as the new instrument of peace and extolling the theory of the depreciation of power in international politics. Still, Wilson sent American forces to Mexico in pursuit of Pancho Villa and to Russia to quell the October Revolution. Idealist theory looked once more far removed from the realities of world politics.

At one time, the idealists clashed with the power theorists, accusing them of cynicism, of making success the standard of political action, and of indifference to moral criteria in foreign policy.

After World War II, idealism took a rather sharp turn. It became the ideological flag of the anticommunist camp, whose proponents endowed it with a crusading Christian spirit and a messianic mission. ("Providence" was systematically invoked in the Truman Doctrine and similar proclamations.)

The basic assumption of postwar idealism is that foreign policy should be dictated by noble ideas and moral principles, specifically those produced by the Judeo-Christian tradition. The ultimate goal of nations should be a rational and moral world order based on universally valid abstract principles; that is, the principles of the West. Thus, idealism became the ideology of Western domination.

A significant controversy broke out at the end of the sixties between idealists and power theorists. Opposing a foreign policy that takes for its standard active hostility to worldwide political movements such as Jacobinism, liberalism, or communism because such an approach confuses the sphere of philosophical or moral judgment with that of political action, Morgenthau stated that "the only standard by which a sound foreign policy must be informed is not moral and philosophic opposition to Communism as such, but the bearing a particular communism in a particular country has upon the interests of the United States."[12]

Although the influence of idealism in the field of international relations has substantially decreased, it has recently made a vigorous comeback in the guise of *neoconservatism*. Again, international politics is viewed as a clash of ideas and values, the stake being Western domination. According to a leading protagonist, Daniel P. Moynihan, the greatest influence in the Third World is neither the Soviet nor the American model but British socialism of the Fabian variety, an ideology that is inherently anti-American and anticapitalist. This ideology seeks to increase wealth not through expanded production but through redistribution of existing wealth. Rejecting the argument of Third World leaders that the present international order is exploitative and that it functions to preserve the economic domination of the West, Moynihan holds that the disparity in wealth has arisen because the United States is an efficient producer, whereas the state-run economies of most developing nations are by nature inefficient. He argues that it is therefore time for the United States to counter Third World denunciations and to extol the efficiency of liberal economics and the virtues of Western democracy.[13]

Such a policy is viewed by Zbigniew Brzezinski as posing "the specter of an isolated America in a hostile world." While emphasizing that global politics are becoming egalitarian rather than libertarian and that even in the developed world (including the United States) the economic role of the state has grown considerably, he argues that

> to reduce global complexity and the emerging global preoccupations to the simple dichotomy of democracy (or freedom) versus despotism (or statism) is in fact to sever the libertarian linkage between America and the world; it is to reinforce radical passions abroad; it is to promote America's philosophical and hence also political isolation.[14]

Apparently, idealism now fares better with rhetoric than with politics.

MARXISM OF MARX

The Marxist school of thought, with over a century of influence in economics and social science, is a newcomer in terms of international relations. Although Marx formulated the theory of the formation of the world capitalist system and of the world market and Lenin developed Marx's thought into the theory of imperialism and of proletarian revolution, they did not articulate a well-rounded theory of international relations. Only recently has international relations become a separate teaching and research discipline in socialist countries, and its academic status is still in the making.[15]

What distinguishes Marxism from all other schools of thought and what is its particular theoretical approach to international relations? From our earlier analysis of non-Marxist schools, the conclusion could easily be drawn that Marxism rejects psychological moods and reactions, biological factors, technology, ideas, and moral principles as the primary causes behind, or the determining factors in, international relations. Although each of these plays a role in world affairs, none can by itself explain the complex phenomena and processes of international affairs. Not even such primary factors in society (or national system) as the production and reproduction of goods or class struggle alone accounts for the whole course of international relations and world politics.

One of the most widespread misconceptions about Marxism is to view it as *economic determinism*. This derives from certain propositions that Marx and Engels wrote while formulating their general thesis that the way in which men produce determines the entire complex of ideas and institutions that make up the social order. Critics who label Marxism economic determinism as well as deterministic Marxists themselves choose to consider in isolation this thesis on the decisive role of the mode of production. At the same time they totally neglect Marx's thesis regarding its dialectical interaction with the other factors—political, social, and ideological—at work in society. A similarly mechanistic interpretation is made of Marx's theory of base and superstructure. Thus, only the first part of this theory—namely, that the base, which is material, determines the superstructure, which is intellectual, cultural, and political—is considered. The second part, that is, the reverse action of the superstructure upon the base, is overlooked. In other words, the idea that the superstructure is in a general way the product of the base does not mean that the superstructure is merely a passive, neutral reflection of the base. On the contrary, once the superstructure takes shape, it becomes a very active force: political ideas and institutions assist the base in coming into being and in consolidating itself. Briefly, Marx's classic formula that "it is not the consciousness of men that determines their existence, but on the contrary, it is the social existence that determines their consciousness" is grossly falsified if not immediately coupled with Marx's thesis concerning the reverse influence of social consciousness on the development of social existence. It is only by understanding this dialectical interaction between the mode of production of material life and the sociopolitical factors in society, between base and superstructure, or between social existence and social consciousness that one can grasp the fundamental message of Marxism: all philosophies have sought to explain the world; the point, however, is to change it (Marx's *Theses on Feuerbach*). That is, Marxist philosophy is supposed to change the world. Lenin translated this philosophical message into a political guideline: there is no revolutionary action without revolutionary theory.

Perhaps in no other social science besides international relations is correct understanding of the dialectical interaction between economic and other factors (political, military, ideological, etc.) so essential. For if it is true in general that social phenomena cannot be explained as the mechanical and direct result of the mode of production, then narrow economic materialism is more absurd and misleading in international relations than anywhere else.

Truly enough, the identification of Marxism with economic determinism has been made more than once by proponents of Marxism. Stalin himself was a champion of economic determinism: his claim that the transformation of the Soviet Union into a communist society was predicated on the attainment of a certain level of industrial output must be considered a classic of the genre.[16]

Marx and Engels repeatedly warned against narrow economic determinism. In this regard Engels emphasized that

> according to the materialist conception of history, the production and reproduction in real life is the *ultimately* determining element in history. More than this neither Marx nor I have ever asserted. Hence, if somebody twists this into saying that the economic element is the only determining one, he transforms that proposition into a meaningless, abstract, and absurd phrase. The economic situation is the base, but the various elements of the superstructure—political, juridical, philosophical, theories, religious views and their further development into systems of dogmas, also exercise their influence upon the course of the historical struggles and in many cases preponderate in determining their form. There is an interaction of all those elements in which, amid all the endless hosts of accidents, the economic movement finally asserts itself as necessary.[17]

This statement puts the matter in proper perspective. Indeed, if the economic element alone were determinative, then why the whole theory of class struggle and of social revolution? There would be nothing for the working class to do except to await the denouement of the historical process of which it would be the ultimate beneficiary.

Let us now turn to international relations. We shall have to recognize that on the international level even the role played by the mode of production is different from that in society. Indeed, we cannot apply Marx's theory regarding the relationship between base and superstructure in national settings to the international arena, where there is neither a base nor a superstructure as a unitary whole as long as productive relations function within national economies. Therefore, the relationship between the two works vertically within national societies and not horizontally from one nation to another. Thus, radical changes in the base of a particular country—for example, East Germany, whose economy is socialist—do not directly affect the superstructure of other (including neighboring) nations— West Germany—although the two German states formed a single national unit before World War II.

The logical conclusion is that the decisive role of the economic factor in international relations must be conceived differently from that in national society. In international relations, the best definition of the economic factor that I know is the metaphor once used by Engels: the red thread that runs through all other relations (political, ideological, juridical, military, etc.) and helps explain their character. To illustrate this, any researcher attempting to explain the Vietnam war in economic terms is bound to fail. Obviously, political and strategic factors prevailed in that case. However, one could not satisfactorily explain the political action of military intervention in Southeast Asia except in the context of a historical, expansionist drive on the part of a mighty industrial and financial power. As James Chace put it, "since its inception the United States has been unafraid to exercise power in world affairs." He illustrated this point with the fact that the United States used its armed forces abroad 159 times from 1798 to 1945.[18] Like England, which discovered its maritime vocation only after the industrial revolution, so the United States discovered its Manifest Destiny only after it had accumulated sufficient economic power to support overseas expansion.

In a sense, the technological school (earlier mentioned in this chapter) is a vulgarization of economism, a reductionist view of world dynamics. While it is evident that modern technology has radically transformed the environment in which international politics is conducted, it should be equally evident that technology does not make policy, so to speak, with its own hands. Therefore, it is fallacious to establish a direct relationship between international events, say, the French Revolution or the Peace of Vienna, and key inventions of the historical period.19

Of course, Marxism has always emphasized the primary impact of material production (including inventions and in general technology) on the development of society. However, for a Marxist, production or technology has no direct access to politics but acts only through intermediary social layers such as social groups, classes, and nations. Historical events like the French Revolution occur only as a consequence of the profound changes that new productive forces and inventions generate in the class situation and in the relationship of forces among social classes. Also, the Peace of Vienna was not the direct result of either the steam engine or the artillery shell but rather the temporary resolution (reached by diplomats and governments) of a series of interclass and international conflicts. Unquestionably, both industrial and military inventions played a significant role in the power buildup of the major European states and in the outcome of their rivalry, but the impact of these factors on politics was felt through an intermediate social layer: classes and nations. Today also, nuclear technology does not engender nuclear policy by itself. There are nations that possess nuclear facilities and know-how and refuse to make the bomb, whereas other nations at a preindustrial stage have made tremendous efforts and sacrifices to acquire nuclear weapons. To sum up this point, the primary role of the economic factor in international relations must always be viewed in its dialectical relationship with political, social, military, and ideological factors and properly assessed in each individual situation and case.

In this chapter, I have dealt with the Marxist answer to the question of the decisive factor. Additional major lines of inquiry in Marxist theory that are relevant to international relations constitute the focus of this volume and, therefore, I am not going to tackle them here and now.

The only point that should be made here is that other schools of thought in one way or another take the existing system for granted, search for harmonies of interest among contending classes and nations, and discover tendencies toward stability and equilibrium, assuming that change is or should be gradual and peaceful. However, the basic message of Marxism today is that the world in which we live is not one of harmonies of interest and tendencies toward stability and peaceful change but rather one dominated by conflicts of interest, tendencies toward instability, and recurring breaks in the continuity of historical development.

Lastly, Marx's theories and method were based on the most advanced scientific discoveries and philosophical systems of his time. Marxists nowadays must keep abreast of recent contributions to science and thought, examine them discriminatingly, test their explanatory power against contemporary social reality, and eventually integrate those that stand the test into Marxist theory and methodology, thus bringing Marxism up to date. To do so is imperative for a theory that wants to remain relevant more than a century after its formulation. Staying in touch with recent developments is particularly vital in the study of international relations, where most new concepts and methods of inquiry and analysis have been elaborated and applied *outside* the Marxist school. Accordingly, my approach in the following chapters is guided by this imperative.

NOTES

1. Thomas Hobbes, *Leviathan* (Oxford: Blackwell, 1957), p. 82.
2. Pierre Renouvin, ed. *Histoire des relations internationales*, 3d ed. (Paris: Hachette, 1964).
3. See Jean-Baptiste Duroselle, "Les forces profondes," in *Etudes d'histoire des relations internationales*, ed. Pierre Renouvin (Paris: Presses universitaires de France, 1966).
4. Renouvin, *Histoire des relations internationales*, General Introduction.
5. See Herbert Kelman, *International Behavior* (New York: Holt, 1965); Otto Klineberg, *The Human Dimension in International Relations* (New York: Holt, 1964); Jerome Frank, *Sanity and Survival* (New York: Random House, Vintage, 1967).
6. David Easton, "The New Revolution in Political Science," *American Political Science Review*, no. 4 (1969): 1052.
7. See Richard Snyder, *Foreign Policy Decision-Making* (New York: Free Press, 1962).
8. Kelman, op. cit., p. 7.
9. Hans J. Morgenthau, *Politics among Nations*, 4th ed. (New York: Knopf, 1967), pp. 32-33.
10. Harold Sprout and Margaret Sprout, *Foundations of International Politics* (Princeton: Van Nostrand, 1966), pp. 212-213.
11. Ibid., p. 226.
12. Hans J. Morgenthau, *A New Foreign Policy for the United States* (New York: Praeger, 1969), pp. 26-27.
13. Daniel P. Moynihan, "The U.S. in Opposition," *Commentary*, March 1975.
14. Zbigniew Brzezinski, "Specter of an Isolated U.S. in a Hostile World," *Foreign Policy*, Summer 1976.
15. In 1969, a large symposium took place in the Soviet Union on the necessity of elaborating a Marxist theory of international relations. In his opening statement, N. N. Inozemtsev emphasized the need for clarifying the subject-

matter and methodology of this new field, determining its place in the system of social sciences, and defining its categories and concepts. N. N. Inozemtsev, "Problems in the Theory of International Relations," *Mirovaia ekonomika i mezdunarodniye otnosheniye* (Moscow), no. 9 (1969); 88-106.

16. I. V. Stalin, Speech before the electorate, 9 February 1946 (Bucharest: Ed. P.L.P., 1946).

17. K. Marx and F. Engels, *Selected Works* (Moscow: Foreign Languages Publishing House, 1950), 1: 443-444.

18. James Chace, "U.S. Interventionism," *International Herald Tribune*, 24 September 1976.

19. See Sprout and Sprout, op. cit., p. 226.

2. Classes and Ethnic Communities: From Tribes to Nations

IN INTERNATIONAL STUDIES, the concept of nation or nation-state has been the most meaningful and fruitful in explaining patterns of behavior, orientations, events, policies, and strategies in world poli-tics. At a time when the multiplicity and complexity of actors, factors, and variables in the international arena overwhelm and baffle the international relations student, the role of nations in world politics is a safe reference point that prevents him from getting lost.

Yet, our working knowledge of nations is fairly poor. To a large extent, the conflicts, tensions, and misunderstandings that mark the modern world are engendered by wrong or inadequate evaluations of the concept and the reality of the nation, of its vital and dynamic force, of its inner and outer dialectical motion, and of its organic physiology and development. In the West, theories of both conflict and integration grossly underestimate the vitality and dynamism of nations; thus, the fortunes of Quebec and Ulster, Scottish nation-alism, the "ethnic revival" in the United States, not to mention the vagaries of the European Economic Community (EEC), are puzzling phenomena. In the East, ever since the *Communist Manifesto* proved wrong in its anticipation that national differences and antagonisms between peoples will vanish owing to the development of the bour-geoisie,[1] theoretical mistakes regarding nations and nationalism have been piling up. On top of this came Stalin's blunder as he asserted in 1952 that the bourgeoisie had discarded the banner of national independence and sold out the rights and independence of the nation for dollars.[2] Only a few years after that statement the whole world witnessed President de Gaulle's policy of independence and later Japan's opposition to the "Nixon shocks" designed to strengthen the relative position of the dollar.

15

Therefore, the study of the nation as a concept and a living reality is our starting point.

THE WEAK POINT OF MARXISM AND LENINISM

In Latin, "nation" has a broader meaning than it has in modern political science; it refers to the division of human kind into a series of distinct *ethnic communities*. Indeed, to understand what modern nations are, one has to examine earlier types of ethnic communities to determine whether and how they differ from later types.

In Marxist literature, the ethnic community is one of the blank spots. Marx and Engels focused exclusively on the class struggle, its historical origin and development, and on the state as the instrument of class domination.[3] The end result was their well-rounded theory of classes and class struggle.

The other facet of historical development, the ethnic communities in which people aggregate on the basis of a different kind of relationship—initially kinship and subsequently such ties as common language, territory, culture or religion etc.—found in Marx's works only accidental treatment. And precisely here lies the crux of the matter: the evolution of ethnic communities has not always followed the logic of the class struggle.

Lenin was under considerable pressure to deal with the national question in such a multinational conglomerate as tsarist Russia, the "prison of nations" as he called it. He did so quite brilliantly in his studies on national rivalries, conflicts, and domination. Yet this issue was so burning that it precluded the study of ethnic communities; therefore, Lenin never realized the qualitative change brought about by the formation of modern nations in the evolution of ethnic communities. Whereas Marx's writings emphasize that various communities and societies based on the Asiatic, ancient, and modern bourgeois modes of production represented historical progress, Lenin's approach differed somewhat. A thorough reading of his works cannot escape the conclusion that Lenin stressed the negative aspects of the nation (see, for example, his concept of nationalism). In this he displayed the almost traditional Marxist bias against national consciousness as something that obstructs the forging of class consciousness and indirectly the political emancipation of the proletariat.

This particular bias generated Lenin's ambiguous position on nationalism although he subscribed to Marx's view that "no nation can be free if it oppresses other nations" and pointed out the distinction between the nationalism of an oppressing nation and that of an oppressed nation.[4] Ultimately, this understanding caused Lenin to extend the discussion of the national question (heretofore limited to Europe) to the hundreds of millions of Asian and African people suffering national oppression under colonial rule.

In 1913 Stalin advanced a definition of "nation" that was widely accepted for many years: "A nation is a historically evolved, stable community of language, territory, economic life and psychological make-up manifested in a community of culture."[5] However, it became increasingly obvious over time that the historical background on which this definition was based was purely European as was the basis of Stalin's reductionist scheme of historical social formations: primitive-communal, slave, feudal, capitalist, and socialist.[6] Marx's perceptive thesis on the Asiatic mode of production was not only anathema to Stalin but also taboo; he explained history as a mechanistic succession of the five social formations listed above. This ideological framework was very convenient: whatever the policies and decisions one makes, the triumph of socialism is inevitable. Here, we must recall Marx's familiar reaction whenever confronted with such mechanistic views of history: what those gentlemen lack is *dialectics*! We should, however, substitute here comrades for gentlemen. . . .

STALIN: FROM "CLASSES ONLY"
TO "MOTHER RUSSIA"

Lenin well understood the dialectics of classes but was less perceptive in his evaluation of the dialectical relation between the class conflict and the cohesive force of national sentiment in Germany during World War I. Actually, he had anticipated that the revolutionary spirit of the working class would prevail and had built his earlier strategy on this assumption. It is significant that when Lenin realized (as early as January 1918) that his expectation would not be borne out and wanted to conclude an "annexionist peace" with Germany, most of the other Bolshevik leaders still awaited the "revolutionary war" and ultimately accepted the Brest-Litovsk compromise only to stop the advance of German troops.

From that point one can trace an almost continuous line of theoretical and practical underestimation, if not outright omission, of what Gramsci called the *national component* both in the assessment of bourgeois politics and in the rejection of programs and strategies of communist parties struggling under different national conditions. Suffice it to note here the recent outburst of criticism in the *Pravda* and other Soviet publications leveled against the strategies of the Italian, Spanish, and French communist parties—*Eurocommunism.*

Perhaps the most striking departure from this line was made during World War II when the threatening offensive of the German Wehrmacht caused Stalin to switch suddenly from "Classes only" to "Mother Russia" and similar slogans aimed at awakening national pride and strengthening patriotic consciousness.

Nevertheless, the theoretical thrust in international relations has continued to be class relations. As an authoritative Soviet historical study entitled *International Relations since World War II*, pointed out: "The main, determinative role in international relations is played by class relations and the international politics of each historical epoch reflect the most important features and specific differences that derive from the repartition of the class forces characteristic of the epoch."[7] What about the role of nations in this process? Is it immaterial whether classes belong to a great power or to a small nation, to a rich nation or to a poor one, or do classes behave differently depending on national size and wealth?

To answer these questions, a brief historical examination of the correlation between classes and ethnic communities is needed.

AUTONOMY OR AGGREGATION?

The prevailing assumption in anthropology is that for two million years men lived in small bands or villages that were completely autonomous. Not until about 5000 B.C. did such isolated units begin to aggregate into larger groups. It is still a controversial issue as to what determined the formation of larger groups—tribes, then tribal federations, and in some regions highly centralized kingdoms and even empires. Although most anthropological inquiries focus on human groups as unique cases that must be studied and described from the point of view of their distinctiveness, it is nevertheless agreed that once the simplest forms of bands and tribes transcended the condition of isolation and began to interact with each other, their further choice between aggregation and autonomy was determined by their internal development as well as external factors.*

*Engels's almost exclusive emphasis on the internal development of primitive-communal society may be attributed to his own concern with discovering the origin of classes and the state as well as to the limited information about ancient societies then available. In fact, anthropological research acquired its major dimension much later in the twentieth century, investigating not only the

Technological limitations—namely, inability to produce beyond a subsistence level—was conducive to the autonomy of primitive societies. The development of agriculture and the first division of labor produced a surplus of goods and an accumulation of wealth that eventually resulted in the formation of the nucleus of an upper class, which split society into classes and led to the development of the state.[8] This internal transformation in turn stimulated intertribal economic exchange, warfare over land and slaves, conquest and subjugation of defeated tribes and villages by the victor, and ultimately the need for strong, centralized states to control the new, larger political units, to extract taxes, and to build up military forces.

This fundamental line of development was altered in various regions and continents by specific geographic conditions. For example, in the Amazon basin, where extensive, unbroken forests provided almost unlimited agricultural land, villages were numerous and widely separated; warfare was waged to obtain revenge or to abduct women but not to take land. In the narrow valleys of the Peruvian coast, however, a scarcity of arable land sparked intervillage struggles and defeated communities were incorporated into chiefdoms; eventually, entire valleys were unified under the banner of the strongest chiefdom and the whole process culminated in the formation of a vast empire under the rule of the Incas.[9]

Natural-ecological conditions thus caused ancient civilizations to experience different destinies. Whereas Mesopotamia and the Indus valley were highly vulnerable to attack from surrounding populations of nomads and mountain folk attracted by the wealth of the lowland settlements, Egypt and China developed into flourishing, tribute-paying civilizations protected by deserts to the west and to the east in the case of the former and by mountains, high, rugged plateaus, and deserts, in the case of the latter. (In both civilizations village communities soon weakened and almost disappeared as state authority grew and as the tribute-paying mode of production came to dominate the whole economy).[10] In the Arabian peninsula, the peasants of Yemen, like those of the Fertile Crescent, though encircled by nomads, maintained a limited degree of autonomy by taking refuge in religious dissidence. And in the Maghreb peasant groups preserved their autonomy by retaining Berber language and culture.

Elsewhere, I reached the conclusion that the sphere of politics began where that of kinship left off; namely, from the moment that kinship relations ceased to be the social regulating factor, politics took over as the organizing and integrating force in society.[11] To

American aborigines (as did Lewis Morgan whose work inspired Marx and Engels) but also primitive societies in Africa, Asia, Polynesia, etc., thus providing much more information and a broader perspective of the phenomenon.

sum up, in primitive societies political power was the prime mover in the formation of larger political units. The culmination of this process was the political organization designed to become the instrument of class domination: the state. Throughout, the exercise of force was the indispensable companion of political power. Since in most cases unification and integration were influenced, if not determined, by external competition—so crucial was this factor that strong, centralized states existed prior to completion of the internal economic and social evolution described by Engels as prerequisite to the emergence of the state.

THE NATION: DIVIDED BUT ONE

The two conflicting tendencies—the centrifugal effect of autonomy and territorial dispersion and the centripetal urge for unity and consolidation stimulated by external competition—appear, in different forms to be sure, in all historical stages. Yet only political power embodied in the state, with coercive force at its disposal, can overcome autonomous tendencies and territorial dispersion. The absolutist state, the forerunner of the modern nation, is a striking illustration of this phenomenon. It represented a radical departure from the fragmented sovereignty of medieval formations and it performed under a virtually constant international armed conflict.[12]

The nation represents a *new stage* in the history of class societies from the viewpoint of social integration. The tribute-paying mode of production led to the division of society into a peasantry organized into communities and a ruling class. The slave-owning system likewise engendered a split community. For example, in the Greek city-state the division of the population into two fairly well integrated groups—citizens and noncitizens—was categorical and permanent: the slaves were actual outsiders and felt no allegiance to the city.[13] During the Middle Ages, society was again split but in this case the pattern of the Greek city-state was reversed: the main producing classes, peasants and townsmen, formed an ethnic community identified with (and often bound to) the land; the feudal ruling class was rather cosmopolitan. Neither a common language nor a common religion, Christianity, could bring together these sectors into a unified entity.[14]

In contrast, the nation making process rests on more than territorial, economic, political, or cultural unification. It also involves the inclusion of different classes and social groups in a national community. Certainly, the inclusion in one national community of antagonistic classes with opposing interests and outlooks in no way means either their extinction or their reconciliation, as history has repeatedly shown. Nevertheless, the nation embraces *all* strata of the population of a given territory (a feature it shares with no type of prenational community except the tribe). As the *Communist Manifesto* describes the process of political centralization: "Independent or but loosely connected provinces, with separate interests, laws, governments, and systems of taxation, have become lumped together into one nation, with one government, one code of laws, one national class-interest, one frontier, and one customs tariff."[15]

Further industrialization and concomitant social organization and urbanization, expanded educational opportunities, heightened political interest and increased participation of the masses in the political life of the country, and more recently the rapid development of the mass media organized and administered on a national basis and used for ideological and political indoctrination laid the groundwork for the kind of communication basic to the consolidation of the modern nation. It is now generally recognized that everybody's welfare is tied to the national welfare. Hence, national integration is used by the ruling class—the bourgeoisie—to strengthen its political and ideological control over the whole population.

By integration at the national level I mean the ability of the ruling class to overcome internal social cleavages and class struggle by strengthening and promoting the common ties and interests of a particular nation. In an ever more resource-strained and conflict-ridden international environment whose dynamics is fed by disparities in power and gaps in development among nation-states, external competition further encourages national integration.

All these factors complicate the task of revolutionary forces in the developed capitalist nations, making their work much more difficult than Marx and Lenin anticipated. While class and caste still operate within nations as barriers to communication and unity, class consciousness may break the national spell only when grave economic troubles beset the whole system and strong feelings about class interests are tapped, as seen recently in Italy and France.

THE SEESAW OF CLASS AND NATIONAL MOTIVE FORCE

Thus, the conflicting tendencies between cohesive and divisive forces that we noted in prenational ethnic communities gave rise to a highly sophisticated regularity in the modern nation. On the one hand, nations are torn by social conflicts and class struggles and these internal antagonisms tend to spill over into the international environment. On the other, national integration is intensified in the face of external challenges or encroachments. In this case the impulse toward unity among component classes and social groups is generated and transmitted through the whole community. The latter trend is especially marked in times of war, as was evident in most European countries threatened or occupied by fascist Germany during World War II. In Romania an unprecedented political coalition was formed between the Communist party and King Michael. This coalition succeeded in overthrowing the fascist government and in turning the Romanian army against the Germans.

Whenever one or the other tendency grows stronger on an international scale, it may well become predominant in the entire international system. Thus, since the French Revolution the world has alternated between class conflicts and intense national rivalries. I call this historical interplay the *seesaw of class and national motive force* in world affairs—as one tendency intensifies the other subsides, diminishing its impact on foreign policy.

In 1789, when the French Revolution broke out, most of the continent's diplomatic chancelleries had their attention focused on events in Eastern Europe: the Russo-Turkish War, the Russo-Swedish War, and so on. The French Revolution, however, caused them to redirect their attention to Western Europe, and very soon the struggle against the bourgeois revolution became central to diplomatic activities. Subsequently, the fifteen years of war imposed on Europe by Napoleon reinstated big power rivalry at the top, while concern over preventing new revolutionary outbreaks remained very strong in European chancelleries. After Napoleon's defeat, revolutionary upheavals, barricade battles, and liberation movements once again dominated international relations.

The contemporary epoch, in which the working class is the new social force in ascendance, has also been marked by this alternation of class and national motivation in international relations. During World War I, the clash between the Triple Entente and the Austro-German alliance was so sharp and absorbing that Lenin cited it as a factor that made the success of the Russian Revolution possible. The national-strategic factor was so important in international relations that one of President Wilson's Fourteen Points presented to Congress on January 8, 1918, ordained German evacuation of Russian territory and welcomed Russia "into the society of free nations under institutions of her own choosing." One could not expect more from the president of the United States.

However, when the Western chancelleries finally took notice of the Russian Revolution, fourteen states intervened to squelch it. And it took sixteen years before another U.S. president recognized the Soviet Union and established diplomatic relations with the new regime.

World War II is a classical example of the priority gained by national motivation and the strategic factor that goes with it. The United States and Great Britain, as well as the Soviet Union, set aside their class-ideological differences to fight the common enemy. As noted previously, in occupied countries, too, class conflicts were minimized in the name of national liberation.

After the war, as the revolutionary process extended into Eastern Europe, the United States and the other Western powers countered with the containment policy, the North Atlantic Treaty Organization (NATO), the Marshall Plan, the Truman Doctrine, and other measures. Class conflict and the ideology that goes with it were again on top. The cold war was the virulent expression of this turnabout.

With the halting of the revolutionary wave in Europe, its center of gravity shifted toward the underdeveloped continents. The West's economic boom reinforced this shift, and monopoly capitalism seemed to have resolved its explosive social problems. This basic appraisal ushered in the transition from the cold war to the Development Decades, from confrontation to negotiation, from the doctrine of atomic retaliation to that of limited war made to order for Third World conditions.

Hence, the redirection of the focus of conflict from the East-West to the North-South system made détente possible. Against this background the two nuclear treaties jointly drafted by the superpowers, the De Gaulle rebellion against U.S. domination, the Sino-Soviet rift, and national resurgence in the developing continents are all signs of the new stage in which the predominant motivation in world politics is national-strategic. Therefore, détente does not mean the elimination of class-ideological conflict but rather the removal of that conflict to a secondary plane, waiting there for a turn.

What is the theoretical thrust of all these developments? The basic reason why the dynamics of the relations among nations differ from those of class struggle must be sought in the particular role played by nations in world politics. Indeed, though nations are made up of classes and other social groups with clashing interests, once they are consolidated and largely integrated (owing to their common language, territory, statehood, economy, and culture) *nations acquire a drive of their own* in international politics that cannot be identified with any of their component classes or groups. Once again, the behavior of the whole differs from that of its parts particularly since the whole is exposed outwardly to different conditions. Surely the fact that the United States and China found themselves on the same side of the fence in the Indo-Pakistani war of 1971 and in the Angolan civil war, while the Soviet Union stood firm on the other, cannot be explained in terms of class interests and ideology.

Apparently, while class struggle remains the motor of society's development and classes in conflict tend to expand into the international environment in search for support (e.g., the three factions in the Angolan war), they never extend straight ahead because in international politics they enter a new and different sphere where other forces are at work. Indeed, the type of conflict (and cooperation) characteristic of international relations is utterly different from interclass conflict triggered by contradictions in the mode of production and in the social structure.

THE DICHOTOMY BETWEEN CLASS IDEOLOGY AND NATIONAL INTEREST

From the preceding discussion it logically follows that ideology, as the spiritual expression of class conflict, does not always tally with the particular interests of one nation or another. In fact, ideology's role in international relations is different from that in national society.

In the postwar years, the habit of presenting international politics as a clash between opposite ideological camps was favored greatly by politicians and writers on both sides of what was then called the iron curtain. To American advocates of the "protracted conflict" theory, the cold war and the resulting nuclear race were ascribable to a sinister communist master plan of political, military, and psychological warfare unceasingly directed against the free world and aimed at world domination. Seemingly disparate events in widely separated parts of the world were intimately linked in a sophisticated conspiracy scheme that could easily be traced back to Moscow and/or Peking. In 1965, Stephan Possony concluded that the war in Vietnam, the attempted coup in Indonesia, and the disorders in Bolivia, Colombia, Ecuador, and Guatemala were all part of a plan masterminded by Mao Tse-tung and Ho Chi Minh for a "tri-continental war" against the Free World.[16]

In the East, the structure of dogmatic theory was strikingly similar—only the villain was different. Conflicts and problems throughout the world were attributed to the class struggle strategy and since war is rooted in the capitalist system and particularly in its paramount power, the center of counterrevolution was identified as Washington, D.C.

To be sure, there is an explanation for this striking similarity. Polarization of social forces always produces simplified ideological images. Indeed, the greater the social polarization, the simpler the ideological model. At the peak of the cold war, Western bourgeois as well as Eastern socialist ideologies produced simplified pictures of the other society. The former depicted the "totalitarian police state"; the latter, "rotten, decadent capitalism." Each system was described as being doomed to disintegrate or to collapse. And let us render unto Caesar what is Caesar's due: professors of international relations in both East and West were in the front ranks of the international exchange of simplified ideological models.

The very nature of the class struggle explains this phenomenon. After all, ideology is indispensable to any social group or class striving for a goal. However great the false element it contains, it is ideology that keeps a class together by common consciousness. It is ideology that makes men act together, fight together, resist together, hold onto power together. *Without ideology as a catalyst, there is no large-scale social action.* And because of this specific function, the intensity of ideological confrontation grows with the polarization of the social forces involved. In the cold war years the ideological exchange was extremely virulent; in the sixties, when class conflict slipped into the background and national motive force took hold, Daniel Bell and Raymond Aron began to speak about the "end of ideology."

Once the world picture became more complex and the Third World emerged as a new political fact, the image of a bipolar world divided along ideological lines into two hostile camps became increasingly inappropriate. In the Law of the Sea Conference (UNCLOS), for example, the Soviet Union and the United States stick together on the principles of freedom of the seas and of free passage through straits; the industrial capitalist nations clash among themselves over fishing rights; and developing coastal nations quarrel with developing landlocked nations.

There of course are authors and theorists who cling to the reductionist description of world politics in terms of opposite ideological poles and care very little that an increasing count of events, processes and phenomena can no longer be integrated in their conceptual framework. Two major misconceptions underlie that approach. One originates in the conviction that ideology has an exclusive class character and scope; the other confuses the sphere of internal politics with that of international politics and accordingly maintains that the ideology of the ruling class determines foreign policy.

In 1951, Stalin's statement that language is above classes—which should have been recognized as a patent truth—came as a revelation. As a matter of fact, not only language but also territory, ethnic identity, national consciousness, national pride and self-assertion are unaffected by class divisions. The trouble is that Stalin's revelation has not yet been carried to its logical conclusion. To be sure, there is a bourgeois ideology as well as a *working class* ideology. But, while it is certainly true that ideology as well as world outlook, or Weltanschauung, are shaped chiefly by class interests and the respective spiritual ambience, a strong national element always pervades both. Thus, the American ideology of overseas expansion (Manifest Destiny and Open Door) differed in many ways from the British (the white man's burden) and the French (la mission sacrée). Similarly, Soviet socialist ideology differs from the Chinese, or, for that matter, from the Cuban or Romanian.

If it is true that nations differ not only in their conditions of life but also in the spiritual character they develop from generation to generation as a result of varying conditions of existence, then any major spiritual product of the peoples constituting a nation bears a unique imprint. National character is clearly part of both ideology and Weltanschauung, and Marxists ought to say so. How could it be otherwise when (1) classes do not exist in a vacuum but are part of nations; (2) the community of culture is accepted as one of the characteristics of the nation; and (3) language, which is above classes, constitutes the most important element of national culture and the basic means of communication in the nation's spiritual life?

It was Lenin who said that the three constitutive sources of Marxism were classical *English* economy, *French* utopian socialism, and classical *German* philosophy.

To summarize this discussion, while the existence of classes within nations is a crucial factor, it does not determine the essential nature of national divisions either in domestic or in international society. However extensive the changes in class structure or in economic or political relations, they do not affect the specificity of a nation. (Sixty years after the proletarian revolution, Russians, Ukrainians, and Georgians still consider themselves distinct nations.)

National interest is as controversial a notion as ideology. What is the national interest and who is to define it? I prefer to avoid an academic debate on the "absolute" or best national interest and to choose (for operational reasons) the way national interest is perceived and promoted by those in power at a given time. This is why ideology is often hard-pressed to explain national decisions and actions in the international setting (e.g., Lenin's decision to conclude the Peace of Brest-Litovsk with Germany in the spring of 1918). Indeed, Lenin was confronted with the striking dichotomy between class ideology and national interest in sacrificing a large portion of Russia's territory and population to save the proletarian revolution. The preservation of the Soviet position in Petrograd and Moscow became the overriding motivation as the eagerly expected world revolution advocated by Trotsky failed to materialize, General Hoffman ordered German troops to advance, and no Russian army was available to stop them.

Theoretically, the task of socialism to create the premises for the harmonious intertwining of its ideology and international relations can be conceived only within the context of a world in which disparities in power and gaps in development among nations have been eliminated. As long as such disparities and gaps exist, they are bound to affect both the external behavior of nations and the perception of this behavior by nations and their leaders. In other words, I reject the cosmetic verbiage common in discussions of socialist internationalism that dresses up relations among socialist nations in a style similar to that of early religious versions of socialist egalitarianism. Contemporary egalitarians speak about internationalism as though national interests had completely vanished from the socialist world and discrepancies between great and small powers had been wiped out overnight: no conflicts of interest, no inequality, no competing territorial claims. Only "alien ideological influences" and "creeping nationalism" (both of a spiritual nature) upset this idyllic state of affairs.

Surely one is entitled to wonder what this kind of talk has to do with Marxism? Marxism is basically a critical, lucid, and realistic method, fundamentally opposed to the dressing up of social phenomena. The discovery and exposure of contradictions and not their concealment is the specific task of Marxist social research. Because it is conflict between the opposites inherent in all social processes that is the motive force of social development. Quite obviously, elimination of basic contradictions—that between private property and social productive forces, that between the capitalist class and the working class—does not mean elimination of other contradictions in national society and in the world.

INTERNATIONALISM TODAY

When the *Communist Manifesto* proclaimed, "Workers of all countries, unite!" the concept of internationalism had a different meaning from that of today when almost twenty socialist states act in the world arena according to their size, geography, level of development, and attitudes and perceptions reflecting their historical experiences and strategic circumstances.

In 1956, the Soviet government admitted in a public statement that in his foreign policy Stalin had committed "violations and mistakes that tended to undermine the principle of equality in relations among the socialist countries" [17] and attributed this to the "cult of personality." Had Stalin been the leader of a small nation, could he have violated the principle of equality?

Obviously, a Marxist confronted with conflicts among socialist states cannot be satisfied with explanations of a spiritual or for that matter ideological nature under the label of "cult of personality" or "revisionism" or "narrow-minded nationalism." Lenin's analyses of economism and other such ideological stances always probed the infrastructure, trying to ascertain their economic and social roots or the international contradictions that could generate them. Such contradictions do exist among socialist nations and Marxists would be surprised if they did not. But rather than face them and pinpoint their structural roots, some authors are satisfied with explanations that smack of idealism.

Thus, Herbert Kröger (G.D.R.) proclaimed that "the principle of proletarian internationalism has now become the decisive factor in interstate relations within the framework of the community of socialist states." [18] If such is the case, how can one explain the fact that rifts and differences among socialist states happen all the time? Indeed, not even the Vietnam war, with the American bombing of a socialist state, North Vietnam, could resolve these differences and unite the socialist states according to proletarian internationalism.

Kröger simply chooses to ignore such facts and goes on his own way, which takes him to the so-called theory of international sovereignty described as "the highest historical type of state sovereignty." [19] Here, the national element is lost altogether, which obliges us to concede that Kröger's theory is the highest performance of the art.

Internationalism is one of the noblest ideas man has ever conceived. Nevertheless, internationalism, like any other social concept, is not something that exists outside time and above classes and nations. In the time of Marx it had a certain content; as the Soviet Union started building "socialism in one country" this content changed; and it is certainly different today, when a great number of socialist states, distinct in many ways from each other, have discovered that to run a state successfully under present conditions of external competition and challenge the national integrating force must be preserved and strengthened. At the present time internationalism is molded and defined by the extension of national interests into the world arena. And the national interests of East Germany, which finds it useful to enjoy some of the Common Market's advantages through trade arrangements with the Federal Republic, do not necessarily tally with the national interests of other Eastern European countries or of China or Cuba.

One is bound to reach the conclusion that the role of ideology itself in international politics is different from that within society. The reason should be obvious, namely, in society class struggle is the overriding factor of politics; in the international environment it is not.

Therefore, political initiatives, understandings and compromises that are almost unthinkable between conflicting parties or classes in domestic politics prove perfectly feasible between such parties on the international level. As a result, we have witnessed a series of agreements in foreign policy that could hardly be replicated domestically.

A classic case is the famous Molotov-Ribbentrop pact of 1939 between two sworn class enemies. Today this applies to summit meetings and agreements between the United States and the Soviet Union, the United States and China or Cuba, etc.

NOTES

1. "Manifesto of the Communist Party," in *Marx and Engels*, ed. Lewis S. Feuer (New York: Doubleday, Anchor, 1959), p. 26.

2. I. V. Stalin, Concluding speech at the Nineteenth Congress of the Communist Party of the Soviet Union, 1952 (Bucharest: Ed. Politica, 1952).

3. G. Haupt, M. Lowy, and C. Weill, eds. . *Les marxistes et la question nationale: 1848-1914. (Paris: Maspero, 1914), pp. 12-13.*

4. V. I. Lenin, *Memo* of 31 December, 1922, in *Die Nationale und Koloniale Frage* (Bucharest: Ed. Politica, 1959), vol. 31, pp. 653-654.

5. I. V. Stalin, *Marxism and the National Question* (New York: International Publishers, 1942), p. 12.

6. I. V. Stalin, *Dialectical and Historical Materialism*, trans. Silviu Brucan (Bucharest: Ed. P.M.R., 1951).

7. *Mezhdunarodniye Otnoscheniya posle Vtoroi Mirovoi Voini* [International relations since World War II] (Moscow: Political Science Publishing House, 1962), p. xxvi.

8. F. Engels, *The Origin of the Family, Private Property, and the State* (New York: International Publishers, 1933).

9. Robert L. Carneiro, "A Theory of the Origin of the State," *Science*, 21 August 1970, pp. 733-738.

10. Samir Amin, *Unequal Development* (Sussex, Harvester, 1976), pp. 52-53.

11. Silviu Brucan, *The Dissolution of Power* (New York: Knopf, 1971).

12. Perry Anderson, *Lineages of the Absolutist State* (London: New Left Books, 1974), p. 15.

13. Walter Sulzback, *National Consciousness* (Washington, D.C.: American Council on Public Affairs, 1943), pp. 8-9.

14. Joel B. Montague, Jr., *Class and Nationality* (New Haven: Yale University Press, 1963), pp. 42-48.

15. "Manifesto of the Communist Party," p. 11.

16. Stephan T. Possony, "Mao's Strategic Initiative of 1965 and the U.S. Response," *Orbis* 11 (Spring 1967): 159.

17. Declaration by the Soviet government, Moscow, 31 October, 1956.

18. Herbert Kröger, [Socialist Sovereignty of the GDR and Proletarian Internationalism], *Horizont* (Berlin), no. 43 (1969).

19. Ibid.

3. National Systems and the World-System

RELATIONS AMONG COMMUNITIES in primitive society developed *after* tribes and villages were established as autonomous social units and managed their own affairs. Whereas internal relations are organic ingredients of the simplest form of society, intersocietal relations appear at a certain stage of their development. This prompted Marx and Engels to list the latter as secondary or tertiary categories of social relations, calling them derivative or transferred relations[1] and emphasizing that they depend on the extent to which each nation has developed its productive forces, division of labor, and internal connections.[2]

Over the centuries, relations among human communities have become more and more distinct from social and political relations *within* communities. This distinction came out rather sharply with the formation of modern nations in Europe.

Today, the student of international affairs is often baffled by the obvious incongruity between the external activities of nations and the kind of society they represent. Thus, how it is that the United States and the Soviet Union, representing totally opposite types of societies and supposedly seeking to outwit or at least to weaken each other, jointly drafted two nuclear treaties that were rejected by capitalist France and communist China on the ground that the two treaties actually were designed to secure virtual nuclear hegemony for their authors? And what about the scores of joint production ventures on the part of communist states in Eastern Europe and big, Western capitalist corporations? Evidently, all these international developments come into conflict with the logic of class struggle as perceived in the societies involved. Either something in world politics overrides this logic or there are two different spheres of politics, each one with regularities and contradictions of its own.

Therefore, I shall proceed from the methodological assumption that in order to understand and successfully to deal with the complexity of such phenomena one must operate at two levels of analysis—the national and the world level. The first level covers the nation-state as the fundamental unit of the international system; the second takes the world-system and global dynamics as its starting point. To be sure, there is constant interaction between the two levels: the second set of variables (world-system) is activated by the first, the nation-states, whose decisions and performance eventually generate the functioning principles and patterns of behavior prevailing in the world-system. In turn, the world-system, after processing the information thus obtained, produces its own, *reverse* effect on the various international activities of states, adjusting them to its general motion.

Consequently, our method will differ from one case to another. In dealing with the national system we shall use the classical scientific method of going from simple, known elements to more complex ones; when we consider the world-system we shall proceed from the whole to its parts for in dealing with supercomplex systems cybernetics allows and indeed requires us to start with the global totality and its functioning and thence to uncover its constituent elements or subsystems and the interconnections on which their functioning is predicated.

THE NATIONAL SYSTEM

The existence of well over 140 political units organized as nation-states and acting as such on the international scene is a fundamental fact of world politics today. Although interdependence is increasing its conditioning effect upon international relations as well as upon the relationship between domestic and foreign policy and as a result new types of actors (subnational and transnational) are emerging on the international scene, the nation-state remains the basic structural unit of the international system. This is not to deny either the vigorous efforts of subnational groups in various parts of the world to surface above the national level and to seek support in the international arena or the massive expansion of transnational corporations and the proliferation of other types of organizations and associations trying to establish themselves as significant international actors. The clashing social and religious groups in Lebanon dramatized the former phenomenon, while the maneuvers of the big oil companies during the energy crisis dramatized the latter. As for ever proliferating international organizations, so long as they have no power of their own, their activities depend on the political will of member states. Even such organizations as the European Economic Community or the Council for Mutual Economic Assistance (CMEA), whose proclaimed aim is integration, recognize that major decisions on economic issues rest with national governments. Briefly, so long as the basic structure of the international system is not altered and the instruments of coercion and violence remain under the control of national governments, both subnational and transnational groups or institutions have no choice but to adopt tactics that in the final analysis will influence governments to make decisions that will suit them. Therefore, the nation-state is still the leading actor on the international scene.

The question is what makes nations behave as they do?

What Makes Nations Behave Differently?

The study of foreign policy formation or decisionmaking is one of the main focuses in the field of international relations; it has produced a very rich and diversified literature. Various approaches have been formulated; a great number of variables, dependent and independent, have been identified; and a highly elaborate conceptual equipment is now available to the student who wants to deal with the multiplicity of factors and the complexity of phenomena that link nations to the world beyond their borders. We now may safely assert that we know *all* the elements entering the process of foreign policymaking and, as Pico della Mirandola used to say, even something more.

However, the effort has been extensive rather than intensive. An authoritative evaluation of the state of research in this field rightly pointed out that although the inventory of the determinants of external behavior may be exhausted "foreign policy analysis is devoid of general theory."[3] In other words, the field has identified the various components of foreign policy but has no scheme that links these components in a causal sequence and no general explanation as to what sets them in motion. Since 1966, when this assessment was made, the field has been enriched with new accomplishments, including the original contribution of James N. Rosenau[4] himself. However, the theoretical void is not yet filled.

To that end I propose to proceed from the idea that in order to establish causal relationships among the various variables involved in foreign policy formation one has to construct an order of precedence and find out how the whole mechanism once set in motion operates

Figure 1. Formation of Foreign Policy and Decisionmaking: Research design

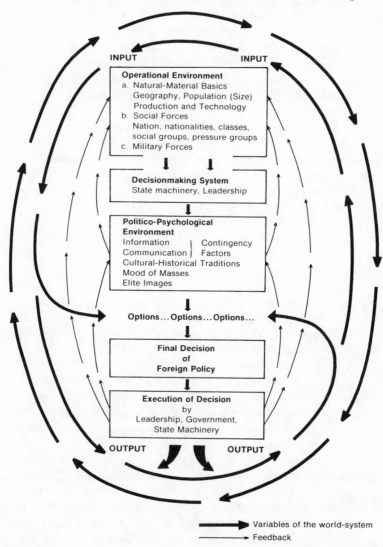

INPUT   INPUT

Operational Environment
a. Natural-Material Basics
   Geography, Population (Size)
   Production and Technology
b. Social Forces
   Nation, nationalities, classes,
   social groups, pressure groups
c. Military Forces

Decisionmaking System
State machinery, Leadership

**Politico-Psychological
Environment**
Information   ⎫ Contingency
Communication ⎭ Factors
Cultural-Historical Traditions
Mood of Masses
Elite Images

Options...Options...Options...

**Final Decision
of
Foreign Policy**

Execution of Decision
by
Leadership, Government,
State Machinery

OUTPUT   OUTPUT

━━━━▶ Variables of the world-system
───▶ Feedback

until the decisionmaking level is reached and culminates in the external behavior of the nation. Since the external decisions and activities of nations are actually responses to a host of internal as well as external stimuli, the appropriate method seems to be to view nations as systems with inputs, outputs, and feedback in constant interaction with the international environment (see Figure 1).

For methodological reasons, I shall deal separately with the primary domestic sources of foreign policy. The five sets of variables are listed below.

1. *Natural-material basics* are the size of territory and population, the geographic setting, and the productive forces. Productive forces are viewed as the most important factor—magnified by the scientific-technological revolution to such an extent that they transform and mold the other two factors into major assets of foreign policy.

2. *Societal structure and forces* comprise classes and social groups, nationalities, and the nation, each with its own ideological consciousness, cultural and historical background, psychological impulses and moods underlying action within and over national boundaries.

3. *Contingency and situational factors* include political and economic crises, coups d'état, elections, massive strikes, large-scale violence, military actions, and war. These influence the intensity of social and national drives and reactions.

In addition to the first two sets of variables, which make up the infrastructure, and the third, contingency variable, two variables constitute the superstructure.

4. *The state system* is the national decisionmaking machinery, the state apparatus, or the government; that is, the instruments of power.

5. *Leadership* is the way in which power is used and directed.

As a rule, the mobility of the first three sets of variables increases with their ascending order: the natural-material basics are most stable; the contingency factors, least. Likewise, the state system is more rigid or enduring than leadership.

Natural-Material Basics. Let us now test the operational value of this five-variable system and see what they tell us about the making of foreign policy and about the way in which nations act, cooperate, align themselves, disagree and agree in the international arena.

To start with, the size of territory and population (i.e., whether a nation is large or small) has been traditionally considered to be an essential factor in shaping the foreign policy orientations and activities of nations. Nations with large territories and populations are bound to become great powers and to act accordingly in international affairs provided size is coupled with significant productive forces. Indeed, if we consider only size, we must list the largest nations in the following order: China, India, the Soviet Union, the United States, Brazil, Indonesia, Japan, Nigeria, Pakistan, West Germany, Mexico, Italy, the United Kingdom, and France. Adding economic-technological potential: the United States, the Soviet Union, Japan, West Germany, China, France, the United Kingdom, Italy, India, Brazil, Mexico, Indonesia, Nigeria, and Pakistan. This list is more like the actual ranking of great powers in the world today.

The missing component of that special status is military strength; adding it to our previous criteria, we are left with the United States, the Soviet Union, China, the United Kingdom, and France—military strength here means nuclear power. (But note that nuclear power depends largely on productive and technological capability.) Hans J. Morgenthau claims that "what gives the factors of geography, natural resources and industrial capacity their actual importance for the power of a nation is military preparedness."[5] And, generally speaking, this traditional view still holds. However, it must be amended to take account of present conditions. For example, the oil exporting countries have succeeded in greatly bolstering their international position, while Japan and West Germany have done likewise owing to their industrial capacity; yet neither group possesses a significant military force.

One geographic factor that lately has acquired special weight in international politics is natural resources. In a world now perceived as finite, the possession of resources that are scarce worldwide represents access to wealth and power: consider the Arab oil embargo and the recent rise of Saudi Arabia as the leading Arab state in the Middle East and as an international financial power.

Out of the infrastructure of nations a major indicator has come to the fore in recent decades: *development.* Apparently, the level of development of productive forces, affecting all other variables, has become one of the most important criteria in explaining the external behavior of nations because it identifies nations as developed or underdeveloped, rich or poor.

The OECD (comprising the rich industrial nations) and the Group of 77 constitute the end result of nations clustering along these lines. Even the postwar division of the world between capitalist and socialist nations has acquired a new profile as the development criterion has come increasingly to influence the perception of world politics on the part of nations and national leaders. Quite a number of socialist nations—Yugoslavia first, then China, Cuba, North Korea, Vietnam, and lately Romania—have declared themselves to be developing nations and have joined various activities initiated by the Group of 77, as well as the conferences of the nonaligned nations.

Indeed, to understand the character of the East-West conflict, one must realize that it has a much longer ancestry than that currently attributed to it by authors who view it as an exclusively ideological antagonism that started with the Russian Revolution and crystallized during the post-World War II extension of the revolution into Eastern Europe. Such an approach may at best help explain the origins of the cold war but not the underlying economic background of this conflict.

My contention is that the behavior of both Western and Eastern nations in this conflict cannot be adequately explained if the criterion of development is not used as an additional, though essential, tool of analysis. I suggest that one must go back to the very inception of the modern international system: at that time the vigorous expansion of capitalism and the formation of nation-states in Europe gave the western part of the continent a strong edge over the eastern. It was the Renaissance, with its bringing together of antiquity and feudalism, that produced the numerous breakthroughs in science and the historical turning point at which Europe outdistanced all other continents. And since the Renaissance was a Western European phenomenon par excellence, it was there that both the early start of the absolutist state, as the maker of modern nations, and the capitalist expansionist thrust established the core of the new international system.

Such were the historical conditions that allowed the Western nations fully to benefit from the industrial revolution, to acquire vast colonial empires, and to establish a century-long international division of labor between the capitalist metropoles of the West, the center of the system, and the peripheries in Africa, Asia, and Latin America. In the process, the former became highly developed and rich; the latter, underdeveloped and poor. In Eastern Europe, peoples and nationalities (most of them still struggling for nationhood) remained predominantly agricultural, their strong feudal structures lasting until the twentieth century. Tsarist Russia, with a state power controlled by the feudal nobility, was predominantly agrarian; although its industrial sector tripled in size in the first two decades of this century it represented at best 20 percent of the national income. In short, Russia, where the socialist revolution began, as well as the countries that the revolution reached later were all faced with the

Table 1. The Development Criterion: 1973

Groups of Nations	World Population %	World GNP %	World Industry %
Developed Nations (OECD)	17.9	65.7	56.9
Developing Nations	50.1	14.2	5.1
Socialist Nations	32.0	20.1	38.0
	100.0	100.0	100.0

SOURCE: World Bank 1975 Atlas (Population and GNP); *Reshaping the International Order,* Jan Tinbergen, Coordinator (New York: Dutton, 1977).

enormous task of industrializing as rapidly as possible, a task of such overriding importance that the social, economic, and political contours of these societies bear its imprint. Indeed, development speaks not only about production of goods and economic growth, but also about the level of education and technology, of welfare and standard of living, societal structure and forces, and in the last analysis about the political system *too* (see Table 1).

Societal Structure and Forces. Societal structure and forces are also significantly influenced by development. The high level of industrialization in the developed nations means that the overwhelming majority of the population is employed and lives in urban areas. A marked shift has occurred in the distribution of classes and social forces; whereas in recent decades the industrial core of workers constituted about one-third of the work force, the percentage of agricultural workers has sharply declined (17 percent in France; 10 percent in West Germany; 4 percent in the United States; and 4 percent in the United Kingdom) and services have grown correspondingly (from over 40 percent in Western Europe to 64 percent in the United States).[6] In Eastern Europe, agriculture still occupies 30–40 percent of the population; the industrial labor force has grown rapidly, constituting 40–50 percent of the work force; and services have grown more slowly, accounting for 20–30 percent.[7] It is interesting that Eastern European long-range plans project for 1990 a distribution of the labor force similar to that of Western Europe today.

In Latin America, Asia, and Africa the industrial labor force still represents a tiny minority. The vast majority of the population lives and works in rural areas. But the alarming fact is that in the Third World industry absorbs fewer workers than it displaces craftsmen or "releases" peasants from agriculture. Thus, urban growth here means both an absolute and a relative increase in unemployment. In Egypt, employment in towns fell from 32 percent in 1914 to 22 percent in 1960. In the Maghreb and in West Africa the unemployed around 1965 represented 15–20 percent of the urban labor force.[8]

Surely, social structure and forces constitute an important set of variables in the formation of foreign policy and in the external behavior of nations. Therefore, the effect of level of development upon classes, groups, and the nation as a whole must be carefully scrutinized.*

*A certain relationship also exists between development and the political system. While in the developed nations the parliament and the multiparty system have become almost a rule acknowledged recently even by Western communist parties, in the developing nations parliament is most often viewed as a "luxury

Much has been said and written recently about how the life-style in industrial societies affects the attitudes of social strata on such international issues as population growth, scarce resources, and the new demand for change in the international economic order. Equally relevant to the question of a new world order is the antiquated social structure of some developing nations and the disparity in wealth between the social elite and the masses in those countries.

To sum up this point, it is important to realize that although the impact of productive forces upon societal variables is fairly uniform it does not tell the whole story about either the social structure of individual nations or the dynamics of the class struggle and the ensuing behavior of classes beyond national borders. One must also take into account the specific features of a nation's political and cultural traditions.

Generally speaking, as we move from the natural-material basics to a consideration of societal structure and forces one should avoid a mechanistic view and keep in mind that the basics do not act directly upon politics, domestic as well as foreign, but only indirectly— through the societal variables—thus influencing the behavior of social groups, classes, and the nation. Furthermore, while social structure (especially class interests) is a fundamental factor in the foreign policy of states, foreign policy is not shaped exclusively and dominated by domestic class interests. Such statements as "foreign policy is the conscious activity of class and its representatives aimed at achieving its goals in international affairs"[9] fail to recognize that foreign policy cannot be, and never is, a simple projection of domestic politics into the international setting, as indicated earlier. What is more, no social class displays the same external behavior from country to country. For example, the way in which organized labor perceives and reacts to international issues in France or Italy differs markedly from the way in which the AFL-CIO in the United States responds.

The theoretical conclusion to be drawn is that in the analysis of the role played by productive forces as the most important variable of the infrastructure, this objective factor, which can be easily measured quantitatively, must also be evaluated qualitatively from two perspectives: (1) in the context of the mode of production particularly vis-à-vis the productive relations among men that eventually crystallize into a particular type of social formation (e.g., capi-

---

item" the poor cannot afford. In Africa, the one-party system is a rule. Such political systems are rationalized in terms of the battle against underdevelopment, for to achieve a significant rate of growth central planning and a quasi-military mobilization of the population are held to be essential. In the final analysis a strong authoritarian regime is thus necessary.

talist or socialist)*; and (2) in the context of the development of the productive forces of the nation under study as measured against the top world performance in that given area, along with all the ensuing effects upon the other variables. This qualitative judgment is essential for nowadays there are developed capitalist nations and underdeveloped capitalist nations, as well as developed socialist nations and underdeveloped ones, and each of these lines of inquiry may shed light on the foreign policy and external behavior of nations.

The student of foreign policy must also take into account national peculiarities resulting from century-long cohabitation and experiences within the same community and its environment. Here, I agree with the editor of the Soviet review *International Affairs* that "the foreign policy of states are formed under the impact of hordes of factors, external and internal; they include the struggle between classes and political groups, the level of economic and socio-political development of states, their geographical location, historical traditions and so on."[10]

Contingency and Situational Factors. Contingency factors are not really part of the national system and the reason they are included in our analytical model of foreign policy formation is that

---

*To operate with these categories, conceptual clarity is indispensable, particularly because *productive forces* represent in this model the *economic factor*, which in the last analysis generates the class struggle and, thus, determines the general direction of foreign policy orientation.

To begin with, the *mode of production* represents the dialectical unity between the *productive forces* (the material content of production) and their social form, the *productive relations* (particularly property) between men, and, as such, defines the manner and method by which men in a given society produce their means of subsistence and exchange the products among themselves. However, the mode of production is an *abstract* concept: it does not exist in a pure state and implies no historical order of sequence, and therefore we must deal with it in the context of society or *social formation* (also defined as socioeconomic system), which is a concrete, organized structure marked by a dominant mode of production and the articulation around this of other modes of production subordinate to it. Anthropological and historical research have thus far identified five modes of production: primitive-communal, tribute-paying (in its early form and in its developed form, as the feudal one), slaveowning, simple petty-commodity, and capitalist [Samir Amin, *Unequal Development* (Sussex: Harvester, 1976), p. 241] Lenin described Russia's social formation in 1917 as a composite structure with a predominantly feudal sector in agriculture, but a combined agro-industrial capitalist sector dominating the economy as a whole [V. I. Lenin, *Collected Works* (Moscow: Foreign Languages Publishing House, 1964), 23:303]. Although the capitalist mode tends to become exclusive, destroying all the other modes of production, this applies to the central capitalist formation of the First World but not to the modes in peripheral worlds, where the researcher can still find remnants of the feudal mode (in the agrarian sector in Asia and Latin America), the primitive-communal mode (Africa), or the simple petty-commodity mode. A sixth mode of production—socialist—is now in the process of being built.

they do have an impact on the workings of both infrastructural and superstructural variables in the sense that the latter may behave differently from situation to situation. Even so stable a variable as geographic location may acquire a new dimension in times of war. During the Vietnam war, for example, Thailand's proximity was a significant factor in determining its external behavior. The crippling general strike in France of May 1968 changed almost overnight the circumstances in which societal forces in Western Europe operated (including perceptions about the stability of industrial society). And certainly, stagflation creates a situation that affects not only productive forces but also the behavior of decisionmaking factors in many countries.

Therefore, the student of foreign policy must be alert to all these contingencies and determine at each juncture the particular impact they have on different variables and the degree to which they stimulate or check societal forces at work beyond national borders.

State System and Leadership. We now turn to the politico-juridical superstructure of the nation-state where all the domestic sources flow and where eventually decisions of foreign policy are made and executed. Indeed, the state alone possesses the function of bringing together all the variables of the social formation; therefore, the state regulates its global equilibrium as a system.[11]

By state system I mean all the institutions—government, administration, and its machinery, including the military and the coercive apparatus—in which the power of the state lies; it is through these institutions that power is wielded by the men who occupy the top positions in each of them. Hence, the state system is not synonymous with the political system: the latter term includes political parties and various organizations and pressure groups that may have considerable influence but are not the actual repositories of power. It is equally important to distinguish "state" from "government." Whereas the government is an element of the state system, speaks and acts on the state's behalf, and is formally invested with state power, it is less enduring than the state. Governments come and go, while the state remains.[12]

According to Marxist theory the state is an organ of class domination.

> The state arose out of the need to hold antagonisms in check; but as it, at the same time, arose in the midst of the conflict of these classes, it is, as a rule, the state of the most powerful, economically dominant class, which by virtue thereof becomes also the dominant class politically, and thus acquires new means of holding down and exploiting the oppressed class.[13]

Even non-Marxist sociologists and political scientists in the West are now using extensively such concepts as "ruling class," the "establishment," and the "power elite." Thus, for the purpose of analyzing the power structure in society they find it necessary to treat certain social elites or categories at the top as distinct entities.

British sociologist Ralph Miliband, after a thorough Marxist analysis of the state system in various Western countries concluded:

> What the evidence conclusively suggests is that in terms of social origin, education and class situation, the men who have manned *all* command positions in the state-system have largely, and in many cases overwhelmingly, been drawn from the world of business and property or from the professional middle class.[14]

Having noted the class character of the state, let us now recall Marx's thesis that both politics and the state enjoy relative autonomy from the economic base. Engels mentioned in this respect that there are periods in history, by way of exception, in which the warring classes so nearly attain equilibrium that the state power, ostensibly a mediator, assumes for the moment a certain independence in relation to both.[15]

The autonomy of the state system vis-à-vis its economic base is expressed first and foremost in the fact that the same social formation with the same class in power may display a great variety of political superstructures. Take, for instance, capitalism. Its political superstructures range from the parliamentary system (England) and the presidential system (the United States) to the fascist dictatorships of Hitler or Franco and the military regimes of Brazil and Chile.

Furthermore, we have seen governments and political leaders representing or belonging to the same class but advocating different policies. A famous case in point is the harsh political conflict in the late thirties between Churchill and Chamberlain over British foreign policy—both men belonged to the British aristocracy and to the Conservative party. Likewise, most corporate businessmen labeled the New Deal as "creeping socialism" although Roosevelt represented precisely the autonomous capability of political power to "detach" itself from the economic base and assert control for the ultimate purpose of saving the capitalist system imperiled by the Great Depression. Socialist societies also have been torn by virulent polemics and sometimes violent conflicts between groups or leaders of the governing party starting with Stalin, Trotski, and Bukharin and including the recent denunciation of the "gang of four" in China, accused of conspiring to seize power after Mao's death.

To put things in proper perspective, we must emphasize that the Marxist thesis that politics is first of all a question of class relations provides only a general framework for domestic politics, its funda-mental coordinates; this of course does not exclude the possibility of political conflicts arising between factions or individuals within this framework. But whereas political conflict between classes ultimately involves the transfer of power from one class to another (the funda-mental issue, as Lenin put it, is *which class holds power?*), political conflict between various factions or leaders revolves around the question of *who will exercise power on behalf of the class:* Churchill or Chamberlain, Stalin or Bukharin, the liberal wing or the right wing, the moderates or the radicals, the hawks or the doves? There-fore, in our analytical model, the variable "state system" corresponds to the fundamental issue (involving the class in power); "leadership" concerns class representation.

The state system is the political instrument of class domination. Leadership provides for different conceptions about ways to use and direct state power in order to enforce class domination. Hence, whereas the state system may be included in a system of causal relationships, leadership may not. The reason should be obvious: given the assumptions that the ruling class is the prevailing factor in shaping the general direction of foreign policy (although not neces-sarily every decision in every contingency) and that the state system is the instrument of its formulation and execution, then one may predict the orientation of the latter on the basis of the broad, long-term interests of the former. In the case of the leadership variable, the situation is somewhat different because the autonomy the leadership enjoys allows for too great a variety of choices and behaviors in specific events or crises (international challenges or imminent conflicts) to be accounted for and included in a coherent system of causal relationships. This is probably why some authors call the leadership variable *idiosyncratic*, which a priori labels the behavior of leaders as unpredictable.

The problem is, how much of an independent variable is a president, a chief of state, a leader? How much leverage does he have in foreign policy decisions (keeping in mind that international poli-tics allows greater autonomy than domestic politics)? I suggest that leadership is not entirely an independent variable. Its initiatives in decisionmaking and behavior occur within a certain autonomous sphere provided for by the given political system. What is more, in a class society the leader is both a product of and an actor in the historical process, which means he is the representative of his class as well as the maker of decisions designed to serve the purposes of that class. At the same time, the political telescope through which the individual leader views the world is fundamentally a national product.

Yet its specific manipulation is the leader's very own. His experience and skill, wisdom or stupidity, shortsightedness, or inability to focus may produce an image of the world that might be clear or blurred or be completely off focus. Not only international realities, but even his own nation's traditions, values, history, or power may vary according to the leader's concept of them.[16]

Did any of the distinctive actions and behaviors of such powerful personalities as Caesar, Mussolini, Hitler, Stalin, Mao Tse-tung, Franklin Roosevelt, or De Gaulle ever exceed the degree of autonomy permitted by their own political system? More specifically, did these men ever go against their nation's established pattern of foreign policymaking? My answer is in the negative. However idiosyncratic, leaders as a rule behave and act within the sphere of autonomy prescribed by their respective systems. When they tend to exceed such limits they are seeking to expand the institutionalized sphere of autonomy. For example, the so-called doctrine of necessity was an extension of presidential authority in emergency situations not provided for by the Constitution of the United States; it worked until it was abolished by Congress. Such legal devices as "state of emergency," "state of war," and so on, also provide for extensions of executive power under special circumstances.

The issue of whether some political systems provide too much autonomy of decision for the executive is a separate question that does not concern us here. What is relevant is the fact that neither Stalin's erratic behavior nor de Gaulle's controversial decisions overturned the established class pattern of their nation's foreign policy.

Actually, every state system provides a safety valve as protection against violations of the prescribed limit of autonomy. The various putsches plotted against Hitler within his own entourage point to the existence of such a safety valve. Watergate is a striking illustration of the reaction of the American political system to Nixon's attempt to extend his authority beyond constitutional bounds. At the other political pole, Khrushchev was relieved of power when the Politburo decided that his foreign policy initiatives had become erratic. Nothing works perfectly in this world and neither does this safety valve. Nevertheless, the state system acts as a strong conservative force.

Whereas in altering American policy with respect to the Soviet Union, President Truman enjoyed the full cooperation of the state machinery, the reaction of the same machinery was different when President Kennedy decided to abandon the perilous course of cold war confrontation with the Soviet Union. Walter Lippmann noted then that "there are strong bureaucratic interests in the Department of State, CIA and Pentagon which are opposed to change in policy by President Kennedy, the same way as were the French generals in Algeria opposed to the change made by General de Gaulle." [17]

The conclusion to be drawn at the end of this inventory is that while the state system, as the instrument of the ruling class, is programed to follow the established strategy and foreign policy of the system, the leadership variable should be studied as moving within the sphere of autonomy afforded it by the system.

A final point is in order here. We have been dealing with the domestic sources of foreign policy, yet all these variables also have an international dimension, which is increasingly reflected in the way people and leaders view their nation's role in world affairs and in their external behavior. Obviously, the size of a nation or its geographic location or natural resources are important factors both in the functioning of the internal political mechanism and in the shaping of the view of societal forces as to their nation's ability to play a particular role internationally. As for development, it seems more than ever to be a response to national as well as international pressures. Indeed, its very definition is necessarily worded in relational terms vis-à-vis the commanding position of the developed nations in the international division of labor, in the world market, and in the international monetary system.

Contingency factors operate both internally and externally. For example, domestic causes cannot by themselves explain recessions. The heated debate in the 1976 American presidential campaign over the actual impact of domestic economic and social problems upon the international position of the United States and vice versa underlined the ambivalent effect of contingency factors. Finally, both state system and leadership are variables continuously exposed to internal as well as external stimuli. In plainer language, domestic pressures upon governments for choosing certain alternatives combine with demands made on them by the international environment.

To sum up the presentation of our analytical model, the student of foreign policy is advised to concentrate first on domestic sources as being primary, to study the dialectical process whereby the productive forces affect other variables, particularly classes, and interact with them in a mutual interplay constantly influenced in one way or another by the external environment, and to examine how all these factors meet and clash within the decisionmaking machinery, ultimately culminating in foreign policy decisions and actions.

The Testing Ground: U.S. Policy

Let us now test our five-variable system of foreign policy formation on the United States.[18] We shall briefly consider whether the five sets cover the aspects essential to explaining external behavior.

The *natural-material basics* tell us that we are dealing with a huge territory whose population exceeds 215,000,000. The impressive geographic assets and immense productive forces of the United States make it the leader in the world economy, with a history in which the dynamics of industrial productivity and the expansionist thrust of modern capitalism, free of the restraints of European feudalism, have asserted themselves as nowhere else and have turned the United States into a highly developed and rich nation, a true superpower.

In examining societal variables in the light of the natural-material basics, we shall use C. Wright Mills's [19] analysis of U.S. social structure as dominated by a power elite made up of the chief executives of the state machinery, the rulers of big corporations, and military commanders. Unlike Mills, who maintained that the three components have equal status, I think big business predominates.

While all these groups are decisive factors in the formulation and implementation of American foreign policy and strategy (decisive because they are in control of power) there is a series of factors of limited influence in the United States (unlike other industrial nations, in which classes figure more clearly in politics) that operate under specific forms of organization: in terms of potential power the labor movement ranks first, followed by the universities, blacks and various ethnic groups, farmers, pacifist organizations and rightist groups, and finally the churches. The strength of these units acting separately varies with the situation. However, they can increase their strength considerably through joining forces, as in the last stage of the Vietnam war.

Elsewhere I documented how the decisive social forces affect the formation of American foreign policy and strategy,[20] focusing on the period 1957-1958, which was crucial in terms of the destiny of the United States. It was at that time that Sputnik—in demonstrating the Soviet development of intercontinental ballistic missiles—produced the "crisis of atomic strategy." Almost immediately, three major groups were constituted, each made up of top corporate executives, generals and admirals, press-trust magnates, and establishment scientists. Their end results were the Rockefeller Report, the Gaither Report, and the Council on Foreign Relations with Henry Kissinger as rapporteur. These bodies guided the articulation of a new military doctrine and made short-term as well as long-term recommendations that have been faithfully followed by both Democratic and Republican administrations and that resulted in the overall military budget's rise from some $40 billion annually to well over $100 billion.

Contingency variables are very volatile. Unlike societal variables, which determine the fundamental orientation of foreign policy, contingency factors are of an operational character. Nevertheless, World War II strengthened the significance of some of America's natural-material basics, particularly those involving military preparedness, and lessened the intensity of social conflicts. The energy crisis had a different impact—from increasing the value of natural resources to reappraising the policy of importing strategic minerals—while the 1976 presidential election affected, directly or indirectly, many aspects of U.S. external behavior.

Coming eventually to the superstructure one is reminded that it is here that foreign policy is actually formulated and executed. In examining the *state system* and *leadership* variables in the United States we must take care to avoid a mechanistic view (like that about which Marx and Lenin warned). Thus, although corporations remain the prevailing force in American society, they do not carry out government policy themselves, nor are statesmen by any means the acquiescent agents of big business. (President Kennedy more than once came into conflict with the corporations.)

On the other hand, neither internal nor external influences directly impinge on policy decisions. Instead, they are processed in the state machinery, and this selection process, which does not lack conflicts and divergences, ultimately produces a final decision. For example, Secretary of State Kissinger often clashed with Secretary of Defense Schlesinger in 1974 and 1975 over foreign policy decisions as did the Nixon and Ford administrations with the Congress.

Note that whereas the state system is programmed to implement established strategy and foreign policy in its long-term perspective, leadership has considerable leeway within this framework. And in the American system leadership is provided by the president, who enjoys vast de jure, by constitutional provisions, and de facto, by practice and tradition, power (particularly in foreign policymaking).

The student of the United States is thus in a position to view the long, intricate, and at times contradictory process of its foreign policy formation as a coherent system of causal relationships. Starting with the lowest level, the natural-material basics—their influence on economic development, social structure, and the material and spiritual traits of classes and social groups, including the way these perceive the U.S. role in world politics—the scheme moves on first to the impact of contingency factors on all variables and second to the superstructure, the final level, where domestic and external stimuli meet and clash within the decisionmaking machinery, utimately to produce foreign policy.

The nation-state, or national system, as a decisionmaking unit, operates at the intersection between domestic influences and features and international forces and constraints. We have seen the domestic stimuli at work. Let us now proceed from the perspective of the world-system.

THE WORLD-SYSTEM

Today the international system works as a world-system in which information is ubiquitous and instantaneous; communication is universal; transportation is supersonic; and modern weaponry is planetary in both destructive and delivery capability. For the first time in history we can speak meaningfully of "world politics," "world markets," "world crises," and "world problems," and only now do we realize that the two so-called world wars were less than global. Interdependence among nations and continents has become the law of the world. Although the dictum that "peace is indivisible" is of respectable age, peace was once not quite so indivisible as now, when even a remote danger of hostilities—whether off China's coast, in Cuba, in Angola, or in the Middle East—makes the world shudder with the fear of global conflagration. Economic relations push in the same direction. No longer the monopoly of big exporting nations, world trade has become truly an international activity engaged in by well over one hundred nations. National economies are increasingly dependent on foreign sources of raw materials and modern technology and foreign outlets for their products. The energy crisis made it abundantly clear that economic dependence is no longer the prerogative of underdeveloped nations. Indeed, interdependence on the world market overpowers even ideological differences: joint ventures between socialist states and large capitalist corporations are common undertakings.

When Marx wrote *Das Kapital*, his global social system was the national society and it was in this context that he viewed the contradiction between productive forces and productive relations, the relationship between base and superstructure, and the class struggle whereby to acquire political supremacy the proletariat must rise to be the leading class of the nation, must itself constitute *the* nation.[21] Although Marx foresaw the gradual internationalization of productive forces and human activities, his writings nevertheless reflect a historical age in which the European nation-states functioned as self-contained social systems whose decisions were determined from the inside (although not in isolation from the rest of the world). Marx's model for his theory of the capitalist system was England, and suffice it to note here that England's budget for 1977 was essentially dictated by the International Monetary Fund. Outside factors now participate in national decisions.

Under present conditions, the global social system is the *world-system* with its boundaries and structures of power, its limited resources, its conflicts and problems; its interaction with the natural environment makes it function as a living organism with a life-span, an equilibrium and recurring breaks in the continuity of its development.

Here we must point out that there are various approaches to studying the world-system and the timing of its emergence. Immanuel Wallerstein, in a monumental work,[22] divides the historical process into four major epochs: 1450–1640, when the origins and early conditions of the world-system, then exclusively European, appeared; 1640–1815, when this system was consolidated; 1815–1917, when the conversion of the world economy into a global enterprise was made possible by the technological transformation of modern industrialism; and 1917 to the present, in which epoch the capitalist world economy was consolidated, generating "revolutionary" tensions.

George Modelski[23] takes a different view, emphasizing the political factor in the formation of the world-system. Accordingly, he stresses the role of world powers in creating and maintaining the global system. Since 1500, he argues, this role has been played by four states: Portugal, the Netherlands, Britain, and the United States. The global system is now well into its fifth long cycle, according to Modelski.

I suggest that the watershed in the creation of a global system encompassing the whole planet and functioning with sufficient regularities as to impose certain recognizable patterns of behavior on all its subsystems is related primarily to the scientific-technological revolution. It is the revolution in communication and information, transportation and modern weaponry that has changed the entire environment in which international politics is conceived and conducted and has made it possible for a global sphere of multilevel interdependencies to emerge and function with a unifying and integrating force. Therefore, I place the emergence of the world-system at the middle of the twentieth century, when major breakthroughs in science started to be applied on a large enough scale to become consequential in international politics.

I do agree with Wallerstein's presentation of the role of capitalism in the formation of the world economy although I must point out that many parts of the world remained outside the capitalist whirlpool (e.g. tribal societies in Africa and strong feudal or tributary modes in Asia, the Middle East, and Polynesia) because the instruments of communication and information capable of unifying the planet technically were developed only lately.

As for Modelski's theory, Portugal, the Netherlands, Britain, and the United States do not fit, in my opinion, the definition of world powers as "entities uniquely dominant in the global system," the Pax Britannica perhaps excepted since Britain was the dominant power on the planetary ocean. At the time of Portugal's overseas expansion, the Portuguese knew neither what nor where the planet was, a condition hardly consonant with the notion of worldwide domination.

The important point is that "world-system" is the conceptualization best suited to handle the new world problems that have arisen in recent decades. Needed in this regard is a conceptual link between the world-system and the origin and nature of these problems. Certainly, development, pollution, nuclear proliferation, or scarce resources cannot be adequately dealt with in the context of the world-system of the 1500s or, for that matter, of the 1800s for the very simple reason that they were not world problems then. And they did not exist as such because there was no world-system to account for their global scope.

The assumption from which I proceed is that the world-system, far from being a chaotic amalgamation of elements whose relations are determined by accidental factors, is based on certain structures and built out of units—nation-states—whose activities are adjusted to the inner motion of the world-system, displaying some degree of regularity and functioning according to identifiable principles of behavior.

The Nuclear Logic. A typical illustration of the integrating function of the world-system vis-à-vis its constituent subsystems is the effect of ubiquitous nuclear weaponry on the foreign policy of the major powers. Since nuclear weapons are planetary in both destructive power and delivery capability, nuclear policy acquires a global scope that transcends alliances and overrides all other considerations, including ideological ones. The Soviet expert A. Nikonov has persuasively argued that the technological-military revolution has profoundly influenced all the components of international relations and international relations as a whole. He maintains that the global character of strategic nuclear and missile weapons requires the creation of global guiding systems and worldwide networks of detection, warning, pursuit, and induction stations. [24]

Globalism in the nuclear era has led to a monopoly of basic decisions by the United States and the Soviet Union. In NATO as well as in the Warsaw Pact the leading powers have reserved for themselves the possession of strategic nuclear weapons and the ultimate decision about their use. Both major powers have stubbornly preserved this virtual nuclear bipolarity and have strained their alliances to the breaking point by refusing—under various pretexts—to support France and China, respectively, in their efforts to acquire nuclear weapons. Both the test ban treaty and the nonproliferation treaty, jointly drafted by the United States and the Soviet Union, reflect this policy.

This basic strategic policy was made fairly explicit in 1958, when President de Gaulle proposed that a political triumvirate (U.S.A., Britain, and France) formulate global strategy and make necessary decisions about nuclear war. President Eisenhower rejected the idea precisely because Washington was not ready to relinquish control in this area. As Walter Lippmann put it: "The United States cannot and will not carry the enormous burden of the alliance and face the catastrophic dangers of a thermonuclear war if, within the alliance, it has lost the initiative and the ultimate responsibility on the issues of peace and war."[25]

Secretary of Defense McNamara was much more emphatic in arguing the case of American preponderance in global strategy: "There must not be competing and conflicting strategies to meet the contingency of nuclear war. We are convinced that a general nuclear war target system is indivisible."[26] And with reference to the British nuclear independent deterrent and the French *force de frappe*, McNamara pointed out: "Limited nuclear capacities, operating independently, are dangerous, expensive, prone to obsolescence and lacking in credibility as a deterrent."[27]

This may well explain Washington's manifest hostility toward the French program to build up a national nuclear force and President Kennedy's eventual decision to rescind the Eisenhower-Macmillan agreement (concluded in 1960) to provide Great Britain with Skybolt missiles, indispensable to an independent British nuclear capability. The Kennedy-Macmillan meeting in Nassau (1962) actually marked the end of that independent capability.[28] (The much less publicized visit of Premier Khrushchev to Peking in 1959 terminated the Sino-Soviet exchange of nuclear information.) Thus, nuclear weaponry creates its *own logic* in world politics, transcending all other considerations, including ideological ones.

China's support of a strong Western European defense system instead of the European security system as envisaged in Helsinki can be explained in terms of the nuclear logic and the global power game it regulates. By the same token, the repeated assertions from Chinese leaders that they have no objection to Japan's reliance on the

American nuclear umbrella (breaking here with the Communist and Socialist parties of Japan) also may be attributed to the nuclear logic. Note that the United States is equally interested in keeping Japan a nonnuclear power.

The global power game, stimulated by the nuclear race, and vice versa, make for a war system with a drive of its own. This may well tell us why the nuclear race goes on and on in spite of the fact that present arsenals are sufficient to destroy the world and kill everybody many times over.* The nuclear logic, as the most aberrant product of power politics, seems very little affected either by rational economic arguments or by moral standards; it remains untouched by the most terrifying prospects and is stronger even than man's instinct for self-preservation.

Briefly, *the world-system causes nation-states to make adaptive decisions to its dynamic motion that the latter would not make in response only to domestic influences.*

One final point here. With regard to self-regulation, the world system has not yet reached that stage because its basic political unit, the nation-state, still has the power to make decisions that may temporarily hold back the self-regulating motion of the system. In Europe, where the most compact network of relations among nations exists, tiny Albania can partly isolate itself from the main currents and refuse to participate in the pan-European conference on security and cooperation. Kampuchia is doing something of that sort in Asia, and even within the Common Market, France and Italy have lately taken steps to protect their agriculture and particular industries from excessive imports. Finally, in early 1977, Saudi Arabia decided to raise the price of its oil only 5 percent although the rest of OPEC voted a 10 percent increase.

The Capitalist Touch. To understand in depth the workings of the world-system, one must go back to the historical period in which the expansion of capitalism coincided with the making of modern nations in Europe. In other words, the regularities and behaviors prevailing in this system originated in that historical symbiosis and bear its mark.

The capitalist mode of production gave an impetus to the worldwide expansion of trade and to the establishment of the world

---

*SIPRI (Yearbook 1975) assessed the nuclear arsenals of the two superpowers as equivalent to more than a million Hiroshima bombs. The United States alone has a nuclear stockpile that measured by Hiroshima casualties represents a potential overkill capability twelve times the present world population. (Inga Thorsson, "Arms Reduction," in *Reshaping the International Order,* Jan Tinbergen, Coordinator (New York: Dutton, 1976), p. 295.)

market, overcoming the isolation of countries and continents typical of the Middle Ages and feudalism. It was capitalism that created an international monetary system and set up the rules of international trade and monetary exchange, including the international institutions and organizations that ensure the functioning of these activities. Nevertheless, these developments did not occur in an atmosphere free of conflicts and crises, territorial conquests, and bloody wars. It is in this sense that the *Communist Manifesto* singled out the revolutionary role of the bourgeoisie: the rapid improvement of all instruments of production and means of communication draws all, even the most barbarian, nations into civilization; it compels all nations, on pain of extinction, to adopt the bourgeois mode of production; it compels them to introduce what it calls civilization into their midst, that is, to become bourgeois themselves. In one word, it creates a world after its own image. [29]

Until the 1917 Revolution in Russia, the capitalist mode of production was predominant and all-encompassing (feudal and tribal remnants being minimal); its laws and behavior determined the basic pattern of international economic relations. The emergence of the first socialist state—the Soviet Union, which dropped out of the capitalist system—produced a breakthrough in the international system. After World War II, the extension of the socialist revolution into Eastern Europe, Asia, and Cuba led to the establishment of a second international socioeconomic subsystem.

What effect did this change have on the international system? In answering this question, one must proceed from the proposition that the international system is the final result of the forces operating both across and within its subsystems in accordance with the structure, capabilities, and power relations prevailing in the global system. As a rule, the structure consists of the most fundamental and stable relations of the system and as such generates and feeds the main functions of the system. In the international system, the structure is constituted by nation-states or national subsystems, and the latter represent its most stable, long-lived components.

At a higher level, international subsystems are organized and function on the basis of particular types of relations (military, economic, political, or ideological) starting from regional ones such as military alliances (NATO and the Warsaw Pact), economic groupings (the EEC, CMEA, and OECD), and political organizations (the Organization of American States—OAS—and the Organization of Arab Unity—OAU) and reaching worldwide scope. The socialist countries form a major world subsystem on the basis of their common socioeconomic formation and ideology. In recent decades, as a result of the breakdown of colonial empires and of the battle initiated by the newly emerging states in Africa, Asia, and Latin America, a new world subsystem formed: the Third World.

Regional and world subsystems revolve around relations less stable and cohesive than those embodied in national subsystems. For example, France withdrew its military forces from NATO; Albania pulled out of the Warsaw Pact; Yugoslavia and China, though socialist nations, consider themselves to belong to the Third World; and Romania, a member of the CMEA and of the Warsaw Pact, has joined the Group of 77. All these changes and shifts were the direct result of decisions made by sovereign nation-states. Therefore, one may conclude that with the emergence of a world socialist subsystem, although the capabilities and power relations within the world-system have changed significantly, the structure of the system based on nation-states has remained basically unaltered. And so has the pattern of behavior in the international system resulting from differences in power and development among nations.

What are the theoretical implications of this new situation for Marxists? At a 1969 symposium on the theory of international relations V. Gantman remarked:

> In my opinion, the relations between the two socioeconomic systems in the world arena, if we may put it that way, run deeper than the system of international relations, inasmuch as the struggle between these two systems is not waged only in the sphere of international relations.[30]

This raises a very interesting question: is it possible for a subsystem to run deeper than the system of which it is a part? Let us scrutinize this question and its implications. A system, to start with, may function as such only if and so long as its parts or subsystems adjust their activities to the inner motion of the system.

It is precisely the necessity to deal successfully with such complex phenomena in world politics that leads me to the conclusion that Marxist research today must operate at two levels of analysis: the national and the world level. Gantman's thesis is valid at the national level only in the sense that at this level class struggle is the overriding motive force. Once the boundaries of the national subsystem are transgressed, class interests enter a new and different political sphere in which other factors are at work, adjusting domestic forces to the regularities and behaviors prevailing in the world-system. It is only on the basis of such a theoretical approach that one can explain the behavior of socialist nations in world politics, the differences and conflicts among them.

Radical transformations at the national level have not fundamentally changed the international system, its institutions, its behavior or for that matter the nature of relations among socialist nations themselves. Lenin was aware that the triumph of revolution in a single country did not imply radical change in the international system, and, as he put it, only its triumph "at least in several advanced countries" could make socialism "capable of exercising a decisive influence upon world politics as a whole." [31] In other words, the triumph of revolution in the weakest links of the imperialist chain, to use Lenin's phrasing, could not possibly produce the qualitative transformation of relations among nations that Marx had anticipated so long as the citadels of capitalism remained standing.

In plain language, the core of capitalism, which has transmitted its own functioning principles and patterns of behavior to the relations among nations, has survived the great revolutionary sweep in the aftermath of World Wars I and II. Therefore, although the world socialist subsystem has expanded over one-third of the globe, accounts for almost 40 percent of the world industrial output, and is a political, military, scientific, and cultural factor of growing world-wide consequence, it has not as yet reached the point of exercising a decisive influence upon world politics as a whole. Appraisals made in some international communist documents in the late fifties [32] to the effect that the content and direction of human society and world politics are determined principally by the world socialist system were certainly overly optimistic and quickly forgotten. The thrust of the error in these statements was that the development criterion in the analysis of the contemporary state of world politics was grossly underestimated. A world in which the gap between the rich nations and the poor continues to widen, in which the division of labor consistently operates in favor of the capitalist industrial nations, and in which the socialist countries lag behind the advanced capitalist metropoles with regard to all major economic indicators (accounting for only 10–11 percent of world trade and an even lower share of international investments, [33] while the share of the capitalist industrial nations in world exports increased from 66 percent in 1950 to 76 percent in 1970) [34] such a world cannot be described as being determined in content and direction by socialism.

A methodological conclusion of foremost importance is that Marxist research must now operate not only with the basic concept of social formation but also with that of development. We live in a world-system in which the fundamental contradiction between capitalism and socialism dialectically intertwines with deep-seated imbalances and gaps among nations in terms of level of development. This fact is not something that a Marxist can afford to gloss over because development is not merely an indicator of industrial standing: development comprises such items as per capita GNP, labor productivity, and education, including standard of living and time-budget of work and leisure. In his celebrated preface to the first edition of *Das Kapital*, Marx pointed out to German readers that he chose the model of England as an illustration of his theory because "the country that is more developed industrially only shows to the less developed the image of its own future."[35] When Lenin emphasized that labor productivity is in the final analysis the most important factor in the victory of the new social order and, therefore, the victory of socialism is dependent on the creation of a labor productivity higher than that of capitalism,[36] he was actually defining the role of the development criterion in the confrontation between the two systems.

I submit that the concept of development, under the concrete historical conditions of the socialist revolution, is essential not only in the analysis of world politics but also in explanations of the inner evolution of society in the East, starting with the methods of planning and building the new economy and running through the establishment of the political and state system. Most of these features could better be explained in terms of underdevelopment versus development rather than as structures and traits of a socialist social formation. After all, socialist society is postulated as a postcapitalist and implicitly postindustrial society, for industrialization in fact, belongs to the capitalist epoch of history.

Nevertheless, history being contradictory by definition, the socialist nations have made tremendous efforts to industrialize and, as a result, are successfully catching up with the developed capitalist countries. Although they do not mean to duplicate capitalist civilization, so long as the standard of development is being set in the West by high productivity generated by advanced technology, socialism must take over that position of leadership in order to assert itself as a social formation superior to capitalism. Until then, the international system will remain essentially intact and all nation-states, irrespective of their social or political system, will adjust to its patterns. Relations among socialist nations do not and cannot isolate themselves from the international setting and therefore they are subject to the same regularities.

The main theoretical point here is that a subsystem cannot run deeper than the system of which it is a part. A subsystem—even if different in its inner structure and functioning principles—must adjust externally to the motion of the global system. All nations and international subsystems, however different internally, conduct their international economic exchanges and financial transactions according to the rules and practices prevailing on the world market. Surely, Stalin's theory that the world market has split into two world markets, one capitalist and the other socialist[37] has proved totally erroneous. It represents his persistent misconception of the world-system's workings. As Samir Amin has pointed out: the predominance of the capitalist mode of production is manifest in the fact that in the world-system both central and peripheral formations are arranged in a single system, organized and hierarchical. Thus, there are not two world markets but only one, the capitalist world market, in which Eastern Europe participates marginally.[38] The fact that socialist nations are also subject to the unequal exchange imposed by central capitalism on all peripheral nations vis-à-vis the world market is well illustrated by the rising debt (well over $40 billion by the end of 1976) of Eastern European nations to Western banks and governments.

However, the real thrust of the capitalist mode is being felt in the so-called north-south system.

The north-south international system is the end result of a century-long international division of labor between the capitalist metropoles of the north and their peripheries in the southern continents (Africa, Asia, and Latin America) to the effect that the former have become highly industrialized, whereas the latter have specialized in raw materials and agriculture. This division of labor was reinforced by a colonial policy tending to make the colonies both suppliers of raw materials to, and consumers of the manufactures of, their respective metropolitan powers. Just as colonial production was oriented toward the imperial centers, so communication and transportation networks were designed chiefly to facilitate the flow of goods from the interior to the coastal ports rather than to link the different parts of the country together. Briefly, the aim of that policy was to prevent or at least to retard the formation of a rounded national economy based on internal interchange and division of labor. Its result was to turn those economies into subsystems of the metropolitan system. This is why, in spite of political independence and statehood acquired by the former colonies, the mechanics of that historical relationship resting on uneven trade arrangements, rapacious investment policies, high-interest loans, and so on, is such that it works systematically in favor of the industrialized nations, widening the gap between developing and developed nations.

After the first Development Decade, so pompously proclaimed by the United Nations, the relative position of the developing countries continued to deteriorate. During the 1960s the per capita income in the industrialized nations increased by over $650 annually; that in the developing countries increased by about $40. Their share of world trade in exports declined from 21.3 percent in 1960 to 17.6

percent in 1970. Their foreign debt grew at an alarming rate—from $10 billion in the early sixties to $40 billion in 1966 and $60 billion at the end of 1969.[39]

Even the concept of aid has been adjusted to the workings of the North-South system. According to OECD statistics, total aid to developing nations in 1969 amounted to $13.3 billion, out of which only $4.4 billion represented grants; the rest consisted of high-interest loans. As a result, the debt repayment (service, profits, and interests) that year came to $9 billion, which means that the aid recipients had to pay back much more than they received in grants. One wonders who aids whom?

This trend cannot be reversed by glorious UN Development Decades or by the liberal good will of the industrial nations. As an old Romanian saying has it: You don't trust a fat cat to feed the mice. This trend can be reversed only if the existing pattern of relations within the North-South system is broken decisively.

The World Power Structure and Its Negation. Political relations among nations and the way they crystalize in the world power structure do not necessarily reflect or parallel either economic relations and the world economy or the state of military affairs in the world. There are world powers still in a preindustrial age (e.g., China) and major centers of power (e.g., Japan) without significant military strength. It seems that in the international arena, too, politics asserts its autonomy though in a unique way. What is this way?

To start with, let us recall that in international politics there is no center of power like the state in society. Throughout history this vacuum has been filled by various formulae of centralization of power supposed to perform in the international arena the order maintaining and integrating functions of the state inside society.

The two classical models are hegemony and balance of power, with the first presupposing one dominant center of power (Pax Romana, Pax Britannica) and the latter suggesting a scheme within which a number of separate, strong political units operate autonomously and function as coordinate managers of world power while balancing each other in the international arena (Concert of Europe). Both models are based on a plurality of political units, which makes them temporary: the hegemonic power and the partners in balance-of-power scheme may change.

The two models represent the tendency to centralize a system that remains organically decentralized and this paradox lies at the heart of the big power game in world politics. This is what drives great powers towards a hegemonal position in world affairs. The classical balance-of-power model, the Concert of Europe, saw various participants try to disrupt the balance and to gain predominance. England based this effort on its tremendous sea power, whereas Napoleon tried to upset the balance in order to assure France of a commanding position on the continent.

This game is still played albeit with greater sophistication and against a different ideological background. To maintain their pre-dominant position and be able to compete successfully with rivals, great powers seek to build up regional or worldwide structures of power (the modern version of spheres of influence) bolstered by military alliances, military bases, economic and financial dependencies, and other devices.

While in the old times the vacuum of power generated balance-of-power schemes, after World War II most analysts used the *bipolar* model with the two superpowers, the United States and the Soviet Union, leading worldwide camps organized along ideological lines. The emergence of China as a world power generated a triangular model. More recently, the pentagonal model, which includes Western Europe and Japan, has been adopted to explain the current state of world affairs.

What is the meaning of this latest diplomatic balance in which one center of power, Japan, though a global economic power, has no significant military force, and another, Western Europe, is a loose union of nine states with a certain degree of economic integration in the EEC and a military force that is neither independent nor suffi-ciently strong to counter the superpowers in the global strategic game?

Apparently, the changes that have taken place in world politics have affected not only the relationship of forces among the major actors but also the dynamics of power itself in the sense that the relative weight of the military component of power has been reduced in favor of the economic, technological, and politico-diplomatic components, which have grown accordingly. This is not to say that force will be eliminated from the attributes of power. Despite its setbacks and the severe limitations imposed on it by both the nuclear stalemate and by the diminishing returns from conventional war, military strength and its manifestation—the use of force—are here to stay. What is more, nations that exert power in their foreign policy feel that they can use the other means (economic, technological, etc.) as substitutes for force only if they possess the real thing.

Nevertheless, the actual shift in the management of power is systematically reinforced by the obvious political fact that force is no longer an efficient tactic for influencing national positions. Viet-nam is a good example of this development, and the Middle East conflict strikingly demonstrates the reduced importance of the military factor as measured against the role played by economic considerations. At the same time, the new geometry of power reflects alterations in the international relationship of forces and a vast redistribution of sources of raw materials, markets, and gold reserves. Thus, Japan has emerged as the third economic power after the United States and the Soviet Union, and Western Europe as the largest trader on the world market.

What makes it seem that the shift in power is not a mere contingency but a long-range trend is the fact that the pentagonal model operates in a sphere profoundly changed on a global scale, pointing in the same direction. World trade has been converted from an exclusive club of big exporting nations into a real world activity.

Obviously, the use of force has become counterproductive not only because of the destructive capability of modern weapons but also because modern trade, communication, and transportation have tied nations so closely together that the decision to renounce all of these in favor of a military outbreak looks like an act of madness.

It is in this context that one should view the new militant strategy of the Third World nations. In September 1973 C. L. Sulzberger noted that the Algiers meeting of the Group of 77 marked the new political fact that the Third World is edging gradually into its own and that this transideological grouping possesses key trumps to be played in the coming decade's power game. [40] What are those key trumps? Sulzberger mentioned expropriation, nationalization, exclusion of foreign bases, the assets of the oil exporting countries in the energy crisis, and the huge amounts of petrodollars being shifted from bank to bank in an effort to profit from monetary instability. Indeed, these are key trumps that may change even the rules of the power game.

For one thing, the traditional rules of power politics have been based on the premise that a small number of major powers could divide the world in one way or another and thus act as coordinate managers of power. Power politics, by definition is a very exclusive club; though nominal changes in the membership are accepted, the number must remain rather strict. However, at the time of the Concert of Europe, when four or five European powers were able to regulate all international affairs, there were very few sovereign states outside Europe because the colonial empires covered much of the planet. Today the number of sovereign states is greater than 140. And it is not only that the map looks different. The real change goes much deeper: the political activization stimulated by independence and by the touches of economic modernization, industrialism and mass communication have all resulted in a powerful thrust of national self-assertion that is traversing world politics. While it is true that this resurgent movement does not involve power in the traditional sense of the term, it has clearly produced a new international setting in which it is no longer possible for the major powers to run the world, or even to exercise an effective control over their small partners or allies.

International observers have often remarked that in the Middle East conflict neither Washington nor Moscow could impose their will upon Egypt, Syria, or Israel, and the same conclusion must be drawn as to the ability of the great powers to influence Hanoi or Saigon in the Vietnam war and negotiation.

To sum up the point regarding the management of power, today's international system is the most decentralized in modern history. Such a system can hardly be described with the old tools of analysis. For instance, let us consider Kissinger's formula of a world that is militarily bipolar but politically multipolar. For one thing, multipolarity as a concept has a built-in contradiction between its indefinite number of poles and the magnetic pull whereby each center of power is supposed to attract other nations within its sphere of influence. This contradiction in theory may well be tested in practice against the background of the present world situation: whatever the geometry of power, bipolar or pentagonal, one must now go a step further and recognize that in world politics there are significant forces at work outside the geometric model.

Systemic Power. The Arab oil embargo and the new oil prices set by OPEC provide sufficient evidence to that effect. If one accepts a simple definition of power in international politics as the capability of influencing other nations to act against their inclination, then surely the oil exporting countries successfully pass the test. Japan and Western Europe have had to modify their position vis-à-vis the Middle East conflict and the new oil prices became effective on January 1, 1974, in spite of protests and threats. As for the financial power of the oil exporting countries, the least that can be said is that from now on monetary reforms will no longer be the exclusive concern of the "ten rich."

What kind of power is that which is made up of nations like Saudi Arabia, Libya, or Venezuela, which are individually weak, ineffective, and highly vulnerable?

Unlike the traditional type of power embodied in a nation-state and backed up by military strength or modern economic-technological potential, the new type of power can be defined properly only in relational terms within a certain system; its effectiveness in changing the behavior of the system stems from its capability to cause disturbances in the functioning of that system. We call it *systemic power* in the sense that it does not act in every international issue or framework but only within the boundary of its own system; its influence is felt to the extent to which its decisions affect elements interacting with that system (e.g., since oil imports from the Middle East are vital to Japan and Western Europe, the Arab embargo affected their policies much more sharply than U.S. policy). Systemic power exists and functions so long as the conditions of its effectiveness are maintained.

The specific strength of the systemic power lies in the cohesion and concerted action of the oil exporting nations, while their efficiency stems from the present setting of the international arena and particularly from the current state of the North-South system.

Having looked at the various types of power, let us now see how they function today.

In overall power, the United States and the Soviet Union hold a strong edge over their competitors, bolstering their position with alliances and coalitions organized along ideological lines and making for a significant structure of power. The bipolar structure of power is particularly manifest in Europe owing to the maintenance of its division into two military blocs on ideological lines.

Military pacts with an ideological basis have two major functions: one, openly proclaimed, is directed outward; the other, well disguised, is directed inward. The former is meant to protect pact members against the threat of a hostile alliance; the latter is meant to secure a system of relations inside the alliance (its structure of power). Between the two functions, a self-adjustment mechanism is at work: when the external threat of aggression is imminent, the outward function becomes predominant, while the inward one recedes into the background. When the external threat diminishes, the inward function becomes predominant and the external one recedes into the background. In the latter case, the military pact is used to restore order inside, that is, to reestablish the initial system of relations within the pact. The external threat is then only a pretext or a cover-up for the internal operation.

Dubchek and the Prague Spring experiment simply ignored the existing power structure in Europe and the role of the Warsaw Treaty in this context. Kissinger's warnings about communist participation in Western European governments (described as a threat to NATO) fall within the same conception of NATO's dual role in which safeguarding the capitalist system inside is no less important than withstanding the "threat of aggression" from outside.

In the same context, one notes the impact of the power structure on the strategy of communist parties in Western Europe. Italian

Communist leader Berlinguer has repeatedly stated that Italy's membership in NATO is not an issue at the present time, keeping in mind the military strategic balance in Europe. And the Spanish Communist leader Carrillo, though advocating a Europe independent of both the Soviet Union and the United States, has declared that in the meantime he will accept the existence of U.S. bases in Spain because he believes the present balance of military power should not be upset.[41]

In a multipolar world, the structure of power is not identical worldwide. In the Pacific and in Southeast Asia the power constellation looks different from that in Europe because in the Far East the United States, the Soviet Union, China, and Japan make for a four-sided balance and a more intricate power game.

In a game with three players an important rule is that none of the three should have equally hostile relations with the other two at any given time: such a situation may bring the two adversaries closer together. As China emerged as a world power in the early seventies, President Nixon's visit to Peking became an almost compulsory tactical move, and so was China's response to rapprochement with the United States. Ever since, the very notion of U.S.-Soviet détente has been rejected by Peking, while Moscow has become highly sensitive to every progress in Sino-American dealings.

The game with four players is much more complex because a greater variety of coalitions is possible. President Ford's Pacific Doctrine formulated in Honolulu late 1975 rested on three points: American strength (which, of course, comes first), partnership with Japan, and normalization of relations with China. What about the Soviet Union? It was not mentioned because in a four-player power game, coalitions are limited to three members and thus are always directed against the fourth.

Furthermore, in a game of four players, one side's losses cannot be counted as automatic gains for the others. This point should be clear after the U.S. debacle in Indochina. The real beneficiaries of that stalemate effect are the small nations, which have gained greater autonomy of action as reflected in the policies of Vietnam, Laos, and Cambodia, as well as in recent orientations of the Philippines, Malaysia, and Thailand.

The global game aside, power is exercised today on various lines of action, particularly economic and financial. Thus, huge power is concentrated in the industrial and rich nations, which guarantees them a predominant position in many issue areas of world politics. And since their particular assets have been gaining ground, West Germany and Japan play an increasingly important international role. At the other end of the spectrum, in the Third World, strong challengers of the present structure of power are coming from behind to the fore, wielding new political weapons to change the rules of power politics. Small and medium-sized nations are becoming stronger and more active. Briefly, we are witnessing a crucial conflict: the old thrust toward centralization of power is now clashing with the drive to decentralize power in the world-system.

The impact of the world-system upon its basic units, the nation-states, is thus felt in all major areas of foreign policy—military, economic, and political—and as far as we can tell the tendency of these external stimuli in determining the behavior of nations is going to increase in the future.

However, unlike structural-functionalists, who view systems in an integrationist, static, and synchronic way, belying a status quo orientation, Marxists view systems in a dialectical perspective, emphasizing not only the integrationist and synchronic thrust, but also the contradictions existing inside systems that create the premises for change both within and between systems. In other words, acknowledgment of the integrationist effect of the world-system upon foreign policy of states, does not mean that this effect is given once and for ever. The world-system, like any system, is subject to change.

But change in the world-system is a much more complex phenomenon than change in the national system although the law of dialectics is the same. As in the national system, where revolutionary change becomes possible only when the new social forces are sufficiently strong to get hold of power, in the world-system revolutionary change will occur only when socialism becomes the decisive force in world politics transforming the world-system from within.

NOTES

1. Karl Marx and Frederick Engels, *The German Ideology* (Bucharest: Ed. Politica, 1958).

2. Ibid.

3. James N. Rosenau, "A Pre-Theory of Foreign Policy," in *Approaches to Comparative and International Politics*, ed. Barry Farrel (Evanston, Ill.: Northwestern University Press, 1966), p. 32.

4. See James N. Rosenau, "The Study of Foreign Policy," in *World Politics*, ed. James N. Rosenau, Kenneth Thompson, and Gavin Boyd (New York: Free Press, 1976), pp. 15-36.

5. Hans J. Morgenthau, *Politics among Nations*, 3rd ed. (New York: Knopf, 1965), p. 118.

6. See Robert L. Heilbroner, *Business Civilization in Decline* (New York: Norton, 1976), pp. 64-65.

7. CMEA annual bulletins 1974-1975, Moscow.

8. Samir Amin, *Unequal Development* (Sussex: Harvester, 1976), p. 241.

9. A. Sergiyev, "Leninism on the Correlation of Forces as a Factor of International Relations," *International Affairs* (Moscow), no. 5 (1975): 101.

10. S. Sanakoyev, "Foreign Policy of Socialism," *International Affairs* (Moscow), no. 5 (1975): 108.

11. See Nicos Poulantzas, *Pouvoir politique et classes sociales* (Paris: Maspero, 1975), 1:40-41.

12. See Ralph Miliband, *The State in Capitalist Society* (New York: Basic Books, 1969).

13. F. Engels, *The Origin of the Family, Private Property, and the State* (Bucharest: Ed. Politica, 1954), p. 62.

14. Miliband, op. cit., p. 66.

15. F. Engels, op. cit., p. 588.

16. Ivo D. Duchacek, *Nations and Men* (New York: Holt, 1966), pp. 12-13.

17. Walter Lippmann, "The Reappraisal," *New York Herald Tribune*, 29 February 1961.

18. For an extensive treatment see Silviu Brucan, *Originile politicii americane* [The origins of American policy] (Bucharest: Ed. Stiintifica, 1968).

19. C. Wright Mills, *The Power Elite* (New York: Oxford University Press, 1956).

20. See Silviu Brucan, *The Dissolution of Power* (New York:. Knopf, 1971), pp. 214-217.

21. "Manifesto of the Communist Party," in *Marx and Engels*, ed. Lewis S. Feuer (New York: Doubleday, Anchor, 1959).

22. Immanuel Wallerstein, *The Modern World-System* (New York: Academic Press, 1974), vol. 1, introduction.

23. George Modelski, "The Long Cycle of Global Politics and the Nation-State" (Paper presented to the Tenth World Congress of Political Science, Edinburgh, August 1976).

24. A. Nikonov, "The Present Revolution in the Military Sphere and the Science of International Relations," *Mirovaia ekonomika i mezhdunarodniyie otnosheniya* (Moscow), no. 2 (1969).

25. Walter Lippmann, "The Present State of the World," *New York Herald Tribune*, 26-27 January 1962.

26. Arthur Schlesinger, Jr., *A Thousand Days* (Boston: Houghton Mifflin, 1965), p. 848.

27. Ibid., p. 849.

28. Theodore Sorensen, *Kennedy* (New York: Harper & Row, 1965), pp. 565-567.

29. "Manifesto of the Communist Party."

30. V. Gantman, "The Class Nature of Present-Day International Relations," *Mezhdunarodniyie zhisn* (Moscow), September 1969.

31. V. I. Lenin, *Collected Works* (Moscow: Foreign Languages Publishing House, 1966), 31: 148.

32. See Statement of the Communist and Workers' Parties, Moscow, 6 December 1960.

33. See *Mezhdunarodniyie zhisn* (Moscow), March 1975.

34. Monthly Bulletin of Statistics, 19 April 1974, cited in ibid.

35. Karl Marx, Preface to the first edition of *Das Kapital* (Bucharest: Ed. Politica, 1954).

36. V. I. Lenin, *The Great Initiative* (Bucharest: Ed. Politica, 1951).

37. I. V. Stalin, *Economic Problems of Socialism in the U.S.S.R.* (Bucharest: Ed. Politica, 1952).

38. Amin, op. cit., p. 22.

39. Final document, Second Ministerial Meeting of the Group of 77, Lima, Peru, November 1971.

40. C. L. Sulzberger, "Third World's Trumps," *New York Times*, 10 September 1973.

41. Interview, *International Herald Tribune*, 8-9 January 1977.

4. The Key Forces of World Politics

THE ASSUMPTION THAT THE WORLD WORKS like a system requires us to view it as an ensemble of interdependent elements linked in such a way that changes in one element produce changes in the others and as a result the whole ensemble undergoes change. What are these elements and where do we start looking at this process?

Again, we are faced with the kind of question we had to deal with at the national level; that is, to identify the variables linked in causal relationships that eventually result in the foreign policy of states. On the international level this task is more complicated since the whole scheme must be elaborated at an abstract level and since there is very little experience in testing such hypotheses.

Recently, the debate on the dynamics of the world-system has focused on the Forrester-Meadows world model. Unfortunately, the approach of that model to world politics is conservative rather than dynamic. The authors' basic assumption is that "there will be in the future no great changes in human values nor in the functioning of the global population-capital system as it has operated for the last one hundred years."[1] What they actually mean in their Aesopic language is that the capitalist system will be perpetuated for another hundred years, while all kinds of disasters will befall the other elements of the world-system, resulting in their total collapse by the year 2100. In other words, all variables fed into the model will undergo catastrophic change; only capitalism will remain intact amidst the rubble. However, one cannot change all but one of the elements of a system. The only purpose of such an exercise is to find out how the changing elements should be controlled in order to preserve that one.

The key variables of the Forrester-Meadows world model are: population, capital investment, natural resources, agricultural investment, and pollution. The reduction of the world to physical-economic parameters has been rightly criticized and so has the model's treatment of the planet as if it were homogeneous in resources and wealth, ability to utilize capital, and technology.[2] Actually, what we get is a world without classes and nations, without politics. To use our own jargon, a world with only natural-material basics.

While a model is not supposed to include all the variables of its object, it must nevertheless incorporate the essential ones, namely, the forces that make the world function as a system. And, although natural-material basics are fundamental in the construction of such a model, they alone can never account for the workings of the world-system. Because these components are now organized on a national basis and are in continual interaction with societal forces and their political will, whose feedback on the natural-material basics makes the system function, a model that omits the latter components is alien to reality and to its dynamics. To cite but one case, how could we assess the importance of natural resources, say, oil, without considering the Arab embargo and OPEC?

I suggest an analytical model of world politics based on a system of four key variables, each continuously acting upon the various subsystems of the world (although not with the same intensity and potency at all times).

1. *The pressure of modern technology and interdependence* as the specific way in which the productive forces emanating from national societies operate in world politics;
2. *Power politics;*
3. *Self-assertion of nations;* and
4. *Social change,* which though essentially an internal phenomenon may seriously affect international politics if spread over a sufficiently large area or in a region of strategic significance.

Briefly, the proposition is that the interplay among these four variables (clashes and combinations) produces the dynamics of world politics. All four are independent variables, which means that each has a drive of its own; each is an objective force in the sense that it acts whether we like it or not, notice it or not.

Technological-interdependence pressure is the main driving force toward a smaller world whose parts and subsystems are thus compelled to get closer, to interact with each other, transcending territorial boundaries, national economies, cultures, and decisionmaking processes. Yet, social cleavages inside societies as well as national rivalries and conflicts of interest place formidable obstacles along the road to integration at both the national and international levels. The discrepancy between the unifying, technological drive and the divisive antagonisms between classes and nations is still very great and will remain so in the foreseeable future.

Since modern technology has no direct access to politics, technological-interdependence pressure makes its impact felt both upon class relations inside society as a powerful engine of social change and upon relations among nations, under their two main headings: "power politics," which today takes the form primarily of superpower rivalry and dominance, and its countervailing response, the national self-assertion of small and developing nations. This is essentially the dynamics of world politics.

I am perfectly aware that this analytical model does not encompass all variables of the world-system. Actually, it is not supposed to. The model is designed to serve in the analysis of world politics, and therefore I have chosen only the variables whose action in world politics is of major consequence. Furthermore, it is my contention that other variables may be included within the operational scope of one or another of the four and subordinated to the interplay among them. For example, capital investment or natural resources may be viewed as variables dependent on productive forces and technology, while ideology or socioeconomic system can be considered within the purview of social change and its dynamics. It is under these main headings that such variables (capital investment, natural resources, ideology, or socioeconomic system) actually influence world politics; in isolation, they are of little consequence and never acquire a drive of their own.

Let us now deal with each of the four in turn to see how they interact and make world politics function.

TECHNOLOGICAL-INTERDEPENDENCE PRESSURE

To start with, modern productive forces (e.g., transnational corporations) transcend national boundaries and the technological revolution is increasing the scale of all important human operations. The impact of this explosive acceleration of things, processes and systems is particularly strong on relations among nations.

Within the past thirty years, the world has moved into the age of electronics, computers, automation, jet planes, missiles, satellites, atomic energy, and nuclear weapons.

Indeed, the capacity of various nations, cultures and institutions to adapt to so much change in so comparatively short a time constitutes a problem in itself.

Growing *interdependence* among nations is the byproduct of this escalation of productive forces and technology. Even a remote danger of military hostilities now has worldwide implications. Also, every national economy largely depends on sources of supply, outlets, and modern technology from outside. Even giant America must now import over 40 percent of its oil needs, and is dependent on foreign sources of chromium, cobalt, bauxite, manganese and tin.[3]

Elimination of time and distance through instantaneous communication; speed of information enabling, in principle, everybody to know about everything and be in touch with everybody about it; supersonic transportation linking continents in two or three hours; speed in marshaling military forces and in particular the capacity of nuclear-missile weapons to reach any point on the globe within fractions of an hour—it is above all this aspect of immediacy that accounts for the integration of processes and systems.[4]

The thrust of the technological-interdependence pressure is an ever smaller and shrinking world, that eventually, in a distant future, will result in an integrated world-system whose self-regulating motion will no longer be interrupted or held back by decisions of nation-states.

However, this pressure does not always have its way; it encounters strong resistance and even counteractions from the other forces at work in world politics. In national societies, political, social, or economic forces raise obstacles against its absolute advance and such contingencies as recessions, depressions, or wars may seriously weaken this pressure. The dilemma confronting Western capitalism today is the choice between combating inflation or stagnation; very often, the answer is a policy of curbing industrial expansion and investment, which boils down to a slower pace of technological advance. In socialist societies, poor grain harvests in drought years have necessarily resulted in lower projections of industrial growth.

At the external level, the picture is a far cry from an overall and uniform advance of technology. In fact, technology has widened the gap between the industrial nations and the developing ones, not to mention its role in stimulating the arms race and the proliferation of nuclear weapons.

Precisely because nations differ in size, power and development the integration drive of modern technology does not operate as a one-directional sweep and onrush, but as a dual and contradictory motion, generating a dialectical interplay between the factors that make for conflict and division, and those that make for harmony and cohesion, with the latter winning only ultimately.

POWER POLITICS

Power politics has traditionally meant the use of power by the strong and rich to dominate, influence and exploit the weak and the poor. While the concept of *power* has been defined and redefined, and the methods of measuring power have been refined continually, its traditional meaning still holds and is tested all the time in present-day international politics. How does power politics fare today?

I shall attempt to answer the question by merely pointing out what seem to be the main characteristics of power relations today:

1. Throughout history, power politics has revolved around the balance-of-power strategy, control of spheres of influence, and a great variety of methods—ranging from economic dominance, cultural, religious, or ideological influence—to the last resort—use of force or the threat of it. Today, the rules of the game have had to be changed, or rather adapted to the new conditions for the urge to use power is here to stay.

For one thing, two world powers, the Soviet Union and China, have a socialist socioeconomic system or, more accurately, are in the process of building it under adverse conditions when the commanding position in the world economy and in technology is still held by the United States and the other capitalist industrial nations.

Therefore, while the ways and motivations of the major powers participating in the big global game are quite different, the rules of the game are necessarily the same, because they are set by the workings of the world system.

Balance-of-power strategy in its classic format is not a practical proposition today in such a pluralistic and decentralized system. However, one of its old rules still applies. It can be traced back to the original balance-of-power scheme between the Greek cities—Athens and Sparta (so lucidly analyzed by historian Thucydides[5])—aimed at preventing either power from enlarging the coalition it controlled or to assume a position of predominance with respect to the rest of the system. We saw evidence of this rule in the war in Angola and in Washington's and Moscow's reactions to developments in Portugal after the military revolution. This time, however, the rule forbidding the powers involved to upset the balance applies world-wide. It seeks not only to limit the strength of one's opponent or of his coalition, but also to maintain the integrity of one's own coalition (e.g., Czechoslovakia and Washington's warnings about communists coming to power in Italy and disrupting NATO). The entire history of NATO and the Warsaw Treaty illustrates this point.

Something of that sort could be said about sphere of influence which, though declared dead by most writers, from time to time springs out of the coffin. What in 1976 was called the "Sonnenfeldt doctrine" relied essentially on this scheme. The argument that U.S. policy should encourage the Soviet Union to develop organic relations with its Eastern European allies so as to secure stability in the area (in this case the term "stable governments" was not used) could hardly be motivated by a "love-thy-neighbor" drive. Unselfish concern is not the forte of superpowers. At a time when communist parties in Western Europe were knocking at the doors of power, Sonnenfeldt's message could readily be decoded: we will let you develop organic relations with your Eastern European partners provided you let us deal with the communists in Western Europe as we see fit.

The trouble, as a famous saying goes, is that this is a real world and such schemes no longer work.

As for the use of force, the final arbiter of the power game, the reappraisal has indeed been tragic. Once the great powers developed nuclear weapons and missiles with a planetary destructive capability, the use of force and its threat as instruments of foreign policy was in a fix. The new military doctrines of "limited war" and "flexible response" were designed essentially to save the heart of power politics under changing conditions. But with a transplanted heart power politics could never be the same. Strong limitations on its military activities have been imposed by the doctors lest the patient be in mortal danger. Thus, reciprocal self-restraint has been the rule in Cuba, Berlin, Vietnam, the Middle East, etc.

2. Apparently, the changes that have taken place in world politics have affected not only the relationship of forces among the major actors but also the dynamics of power itself in the sense that the relative weight of the military component of power has been reduced in favor of the economic, technological and politico-diplomatic components.

3. The traditional rules of power politics were based on the premise that a small number of major powers can divide the world in one way or another and thus act as coordinate managers of power, each one controlling its own sphere of influence. Today it is no longer possible for the major powers to run the world, or even to exercise an effective control over their allies in the modern, decentralized international system.

4. Whatever geometry of power centers one chooses—bipolar, triangular, or pentagonal—one must recognize that there are significant forces at work in world politics outside the geometric model. I suggest that a new type of power is emerging that is utterly different

from the existing structural one embodied in the nation-state: the systemic power (see pages 61-62).

Thus, although power politics is functioning ever less effectively and its preferred instrument, the use of force, is becoming counter-productive, power will remain an important factor in international politics so long as disparities in size and might or imbalances in development and wealth among nations continue to exist.

NATIONAL SELF-ASSERTION

National self-assertion is essentially the reaction of the small, weak, and poor nations against power politics; it is the other facet of international politics resulting from inequalities and imbalances among nations. The resurgence of nationalism has produced an increasingly effective counterforce to the policy of domination and dictate; although national self-assertion does not involve power in the traditional sense, it has a vitality originating in the desire of nations to liberate themselves from any form of domination and exploitation and to satisfy their inner potentialities (economic, cultural and political) that have been suppressed for so long. The national libera-tion movement has already toppled mighty colonial empires and in places like Algeria, Cuba, and Vietnam it has proved its ability to cope with and resist the most modern imperialist armies. Nations recently liberated from the colonial yoke are consolidating their independence and gaining ground slowly but surely in the world arena. Whereas the system of power politics is functioning under increasing restraints, national self-assertion is riding the wave of the future.

"Development" is the battle cry of the new nations and to the extent that they succeed in organizing their forces, these countries constitute an important agent of change in world politics. Indeed, as OPEC has persuasively demonstrated, the Third World may change even the rules of the power game.

To all developing nations, the state seems the best instrument both for modernizing and industrializing their economy and society and for championing development in the international arena. No other political force besides the nation-state is qualified, willing and able to secure and protect their industrialization and passage in the modern technological era; what is more, state intervention in the developing nations is especially needed to control the play of the spontaneous economic forces, according to market laws, which always work in favor of the former metropolis.[6]

Since the state in modern times embodies the greatest concentration of power, the question arises as to who holds that power in the Third World? As mentioned earlier, independence is followed by the eruption of class differences and, as so often revealed by subsequent events, the privileged strata either appeal to the former colonial master to help them stay in power or act as the latter's political agent. Lenin used to call this group "comprador bourgeoisie." Recent studies suggest that these beachheads of the capitalist power centers are essential to the smooth functioning of the North-South system[7]; conversely, revolutionary and nationalist forces fighting imperialism must also deal with the agents and clients of the latter. Therefore, the battle against underdevelopment eventually results in social change.

SOCIAL CHANGE

Social change, by which I mean the passage of power from one class to another, may affect world politics in two ways: as an internal phenomenon (i.e., when a new revolutionary government radically alters the policy of a particular nation) and as a subject of international conflict (i.e., when foreign powers become involved in a revolutionary process or in a civil war).

In modern history, revolutions or counterrevolutions have always constituted focal points of international politics. They lie at the root of various conflicts, national rivalries, and alliances, and of political and diplomatic alignments designed either to promote them or to contain and destroy them. The Holy Alliance has remained to this day the archetype of counterrevolutionary pacts and from the threats we hear these days from Washington or Bonn about communist participation in Western European governments, NATO must have a similar function.

In Chapter 2 we discussed the postwar vagaries of the revolutionary movement. The social upheaval in France in May 1968 ushered in a period of social turbulence and instability in most Western countries, blowing up the assumption that the class struggle had faded. More recently recession coupled with inflation has compounded that instability against the background of a breakdown in the international economic and financial order.

To sum up this point, social change is one of the four key variables of world politics and as such its impact is determined by its dialectical interaction with the other three. Technology, for example, has been at once a boost of capitalist expansion and a powerful instrument of social change, thus exacerbating all the contradictions of imperialism. Power politics may stimulate or suppress social change according to its own drive. National self-assertion is related to social change in an ambivalent way: on the one hand this movement has an organic inclination to work within the capitalist system, its natural habitat; on the other, the logic of the battle against under-development and poverty brings it into conflict with the core of the system—the industrial capitalist nations.

What is the operational value of this analytical model? Let us focus on its explanatory power (in Chapter 8 we test its predictive capability).

I suggest that this model is an adequate tool to be used by the international relations student both in viewing the foreign policies of states from the perspective of world politics and in assessing their chance of success in that environment. Surely, foreign policymakers must always keep in mind that the components of national power, and national power as a whole, have a relative value; that is, they are all measurable by comparative, though more or less objective, criteria. What counts, however, in international politics is not so much the objective assessment of national power but rather the efficiency of its use in the international setting in the pursuit of a certain goal. As an extreme illustration, Hitler failed because the goal he pursued—world domination—exceeded by far the potential of Germany.

Therefore, the crux of foreign policy is the correct evaluation of the feasibility of national goals in view of the state of world politics. Feasibility may be measured against our four key variables and examined in terms of the circumstances prevailing at a given time.

As a case study, let us use the four key variables to assess the foreign policy of President de Gaulle. De Gaulle responded to technological-interdependence pressure by promoting the Common Market and by supporting it in spite of various difficulties France encountered within its framework. As regards power politics, he was one of the first to see the impact of the bipolar hegemony in nuclear policy and global strategy. Consequently, he made his opposition to that bipolar structure a cardinal principle of French policy. At the same time, de Gaulle tried to enter the big power game, playing one superpower against the other to strengthen his own relative position. De Gaulle was aware of the emergence of national self-assertion as a major force in world politics and banked on it both in opposing the superpowers and in advancing the interests of France in the world arena. Finally, his position on social change was determined by the aims of the French ruling class he represented, having had also to reckon with the fact that the French communist party was a challenging force in domestic politics. It is significant in this respect that when de Gaulle perceived the Cuban missile crisis of 1962 to be a test of power (with an underlying ideological component) between the United States and the Soviet Union, he immediately assured President Kennedy of his unswerving support. By the same token, while he opposed American hegemony and pulled French troops out of NATO, de Gaulle stayed in the Atlantic alliance because of common class interests—preservation of the capitalist system—an objective that he realized could not be successfully pursued by France alone. In short, de Gaulle's plan to recoup France's status as a world power was too ambitious in terms of that nation's economic and military potential. His successors have been gradually compelled to cut France's foreign policy down to size.

Of course, de Gaulle's policy was much more complex than this presentation indicates. Its purpose was only to determine whether our analytical model fits the real world of politics and whether the four key variables may be used as criteria in assessing the orientation of foreign policy and its chances of success.

When Zbigniew Brzezinski warned that "global politics are becoming egalitarian rather than libertarian" with the emergence of the Third World and its call for a more equitable international economic order and that to oppose this global pressure is to promote the United States' political isolation in a hostile world,[8] he was actually emphasizing the powerful thrust of *national self-assertion* in world politics, which can be ignored only at the risk of failure. Brzezinski is certainly aware of power politics in his assessments of the role of the Soviet Union, as well as that of Western Europe and Japan, concluding, of course, that the United States' crucial economic and political role is becoming even more pivotal through recent events. Brzezinski, who coined the phrase "technetronic age," has placed the whole globalization process in the context of technological-interdependence pressure, and surely social change was very much on his mind when he spoke about the paradox "that American policies have seemed to be oriented against change whereas the broad social-political impact of America has been inherently anti-traditional and anti-authoritarian."

This view implicitly rejects two policies. According to Brzezinski, Kissinger's obsession with the big power game made him underestimate the new emerging force of the developing nations, while the counterattack mounted by the U.S. ambassador to the United Nations in 1975 (much to national applause) against the new nations could sever America from the world, reinforce radical passions abroad, and promote America's isolation.

Briefly, U.S. success in foreign policy depends to a large extent on the realistic assessment of the forces now prevailing in world politics. The student of international affairs may also use the four-variable system in the analysis of major international agreements to see whether they respond to present circumstances in world politics and hence whether they will likely endure as one or another key variable gains ground.

The 1970 Soviet–West German treaty could well be described in such terms. Technological-interdependence pressure was apparent in the Soviet aim of developing trade relations with Bonn and acquiring the most modern technological know-how from the latter, as well as in Bonn's aim of deepening its penetration (a new *Drang nach Osten*) of the huge Soviet and Eastern European market. The signing of the treaty was immediately followed by visits to Moscow from the West German ministers of economy and of science and technology, and in 1975 Soviet–West German trade reached a record of over $4 billion. The power politics variable was present in the Soviet drive to assert its predominant role in European affairs, and West Germany would very much like to play power politics once more, despite the handicap of nonnuclear power status. The Federal Republic of Germany, the major Western European power, is propelled by the spirit of national self-assertion to emancipate itself from U.S. tutelage and to promote its national interest, which would end its anomalous position as an economic giant but a political dwarf. Social change, though it did not play a direct role in this affair, was present in the background in the form of the German Democratic Republic.

In Chapter 8 this analytical model is applied to world politics as a whole.

NOTES

1. See Jay W. Forrester, *World Dynamics* (Cambridge: Wright Allen, 1969); *The Limits to Growth* (New York: Potomac, 1972), p. 123.
2. Ervin Laszlo, ed., *The World System* (New York: Braziller, 1973).
3. See Ralph Stuart Smith, *The United States and the Third World* (Washington, D.C.: U.S. Department of State, July 1975).
4. See John H. Hertz, "The Impact of the Technological-Scientific Process on the International System," in *Theory of International Relations*, ed. Abdul A. Said (Englewood Cliffs, N.J.: Prentice-Hall, 1968).
5. See David Hume, "On the Balance of Power," in Raymond Aron, *Paix et guerre entre les nations*, 4th ed. (Paris: Calman-Lévy, 1967), pp. 133–138;

and Morton A. Kaplan, *System and Process in International Politics* (New York: Wiley, 1967), pp. 22–36.

6. E. Bragina, "Role of the State in the Newly-free Countries' Socio-Economic Development," *International Affairs* (Moscow), no. 1 (1975).

7. Dieter Senghaas, "Conflict Formations in Contemporary International Society," *Journal of Peace Research* (Oslo), no. 3 (1973).

8. Zibigniew Brzezinski, "Specter of an Isolated U.S. in a Hostile World," *International Herald Tribune*, 3 January 1977.

5. Theory of Integration

FROM THE ANCIENT TIMES when tribal society was torn by two conflicting tendencies—the centrifugal effect of the autonomy and territorial dispersion of tribes or villages and the centripetal urge for the unification of neighboring units—up through modern times, when nations display two historical tendencies equally conflicting—national resurgence against foreign oppression and international inequality, on the one hand, and the development of cooperation overcoming national isolation and promoting larger unions, on the other—the evolution of human communities has been dialectical.

It sounds like a truism that larger unions are formed when the elements of cooperation prevail over those of conflict; that is, when reasons to assimilate are stronger than desires to remain autonomous. Therefore, the phenomenon of integration must be viewed in a historical context with each type of ethnic community reacting differently when faced with the prospect of losing or giving up its autonomy. Note that the problem of intranational integration within a society that remains autonomous is distinct from that of intersocietal integration resulting in a larger union in which the autonomy of the original units is terminated. Having thus introduced my general approach to integration, let us now examine in detail its various aspects.

One of the most extensive studies on the integration of political communities was made by the so-called Princeton group.[1] In this study, political communities were defined as social groups with a process of political communication, some machinery for enforcement, and some popular habits of compliance.

Such communities are not necessarily able to prevent war within the area they cover (e.g., the U.S. at the time of the Civil War) although they may succeed in eliminating such internal conflicts. The authors, nonetheless, emphasize what they see as a conviction on the part of the individual members of a given community, of having come to agreement on at least this one point: that common social problems must and can be resolved by processes of "peaceful change."[2]

Here is the crux of the matter, for the idea of peaceful change permeates all the concepts used by the Princeton group. Thus, by integration they mean the attainment, within a territory, of a "sense of community" and of institutions and practices strong enough and widespread enough to assure, for a long time, dependable expectations of peaceful change among its population.[3] Ernst Haas is more specific, arguing that political community exists when there is a likelihood of internal peaceful change in a setting of contending groups with mutually antagonistic claims.[4]

What seems to us obvious is that this study was concerned with integration within a political community rather than with international or supranational integration. Note the definition of "peaceful change": "By *Peaceful Change* we mean the resolution of social problems, normally by institutionalized procedures, without resort to large-scale physical force."[5] According to this definition the United States, France, and for that matter the Soviet Union and China could hardly qualify as political communities because none met these criteria in their respective revolutions.

Perhaps it is not the past but rather the future that concerns the Princeton group, and this is quite understandable. For if the rule of "institutionalized procedures" is strictly observed, capitalism does not have to worry any longer. It is the art of the bourgeoisie to have created such institutionalized procedures that compliance with them would keep it in power for ever. Integration theory thus has a definite class content.

NATIONAL INTEGRATION

Integration is in my view an ensemble of interactions handled in such a way that the affiliation of parts to a certain whole is maintained. Therefore, proceeding from the proposition that the nation is made up of classes and other social groups with clashing interests and antagonistic aims, by integration at the national level I mean the capability of the state-power to overcome the cleavages and conflicts of interest within the nation by strengthening and enhancing through intensive communication the common ties and interests peculiar to that nation as a whole. As a result, a large majority of the population will identify politically with the state.

Thus, integration is not a static but a very dynamic concept in which the two conflicting tendencies—the divisive effect of class struggle and the cohesive force of the ethnic community—is settled by political power in favor of the latter. Consequently, national integration exists to the extent that national communities and interests can successfully defuse internal conflicts, whereas the predominance of inner social or political conflicts leads to the disintegration of the nation. Indeed, the United States was a divided nation during the Civil War; in May 1968, the general strike and social upheaval in France temporarily rent the integrating fabric of the French nation. Nor could Hungary in 1956 have been described as an integrated nation, which means that socialist nations also may develop their inner contradictions to the point that they become explosive.

Century-long experience in ruling society has taught the bourgeoisie to exploit the integrating force of national sentiment particularly when plotting or waging aggressive wars. To mention but one classic example, Kaiser Wilhelm succeeded in attracting the bulk of the German working class to his expansionist goals in World War I by playing the allegiance of workers to national values off against their class consciousness. In some cases, the dynamics are reversed: during the Algerian war the French working class eventually turned against colonial policy and the Vietnam war threatened to tear the fabric of the American nation.

National integration involves not only classes but also *ethnic minorities* or *nationalities*. Here, racial or national oppression, including the underprivileged political, economic, or cultural status of ethnic minorities, lies at the heart of conflict. Even within highly industrialized nations, groups of distinctive national origin and character such as the Walloons in Belgium, the French Quebec in Canada, the Welsh, Scotch, and Northern Irish in Britain, and the Basques and Catalonians in Spain have demanded equality for their languages as well as economic or political equality, and have threatened secession if their demands are not met.

The case of the United States is unique in many ways. The United States has been legitimately proud of its melting pot, having brought together in unparalleled fashion so many nationalities, each with its individual heritage, culture and language, into one great nation. Nevertheless, ethnic neighborhoods in New York and Chicago, black urban ghettos, and Puerto Rican and Chicano enclaves persist. The sixties heard racial and ethnic minorities demand equality and civil rights and such calls are still being heard in the seventies. A French journalist dubbed the phenomenon of minority resurgence the "melting pot in reverse."[6] And neoconservatists have taken up the issue of ethnic revival in the United States.[7] Daniel Bell maintains that stressing origins is a strategic choice by individuals who, in other circumstances, would choose other group memberships as a means of gaining power and privileges. This is a rather interesting statement that clearly spells out neither "other group memberships" nor "other circumstances."[8] However, readers of Bell's *End of Ideology* should have little trouble realizing that any other group but classes and any other circumstance but social turbulence would suit the author. Andrew Hacker has aptly decoded Bell's message as he points to the ideological intention: if you cut the cake ethnically, classes become less apparent.[9] Thus, national integration reveals itself to be a dual-purpose bourgeois device directed either outward (Kaiser Wilhelm) or inward (Bell) in order to serve the capitalist system and its ruling class.

The point to be stressed is that even in highly developed countries (where the forces of national integration are at their best) the national question will remain unsettled as long as there is inequality along ethnic or racial lines and as long as ethnic or racial minorities feel that they are in an inferior position politically, economically, or culturally.

Very few multinational or multiethnic states have succeeded in eliminating such inequality and in dispelling the feeling of inferiority among their ethnic minorities or nationalities. Not even multinational socialist states like the Soviet Union or Yugoslavia may make such claims. Switzerland is to this day the classical model of a pluralistic confederation in which a number of diverse communities act together and form a strong and durable union whose cohesion is maintained by consent and not coercion. What are the lessons of the Swiss confederation?

1. Contrary to widespread belief a state can be strong without being highly centralized. The strength of the Swiss union has manifested itself in defense not in aggression and conquest. The latter requires greater centralization, which would necessitate the domination of one canton over the others.

2. The strength of the confederation springs from the fact that the cantons have retained their autonomy and their own languages, customs, and institutions. The confederation has no power, legal right, or machinery to intervene in the cantons' internal affairs.

3. While three general and more or less permanent grounds of difference exist among the cantons—cultural, religious, and economic—they do not coincide. Were the lines of cleavage the same everywhere, had there existed two "blocs"—one, for instance, Catholic, French-speaking, and agricultural, and the other Protestant, German-speaking, and industrial—these monolithic entities would probably have broken away from each other sooner or later.[10]

The cases of Ulster and Lebanon clearly demonstrate that when two or three lines of conflict—economic, religious, social—coincide, the problem becomes insoluble and the nation disintegrates. In Ulster, the widely accepted picture of a straight fight between Catholics and Protestants is misleading for the religious issue is merely a front for the underlying economic, political, and even ethnic conflicts. Lined up in the opposing camps are Celts and Anglo-Saxons, rich and poor, colonizers and colonized. As a journalist put it, Northern Ireland may be regarded as "the last outpost of the British Empire."

In Lebanon the fierce fight between Christians and Moslems also reflects a deep-seated conflict between the governing, Western-educated elite and the oppressed masses, the former being rich and the latter poor.

Having said this about class conflicts and national cleavages, the conclusion to be drawn is that national integration is but a temporary and unstable state of affairs unless social or national inequities are eliminated.

SUPRANATIONAL INTEGRATION

Let us now turn to integration at the supranational level. This process involves qualitatively distinct elements of conflict and cooperation: the source of conflict is removed from the domestic scene to the international scene and the cooperating units are not classes but nations (although as we see later classes have a big stake in this game).

Supranational integration is a dynamic process that is initiated and evolves toward a successful outcome when cooperation prevails over conflict. The reverse process, disintegration, is inevitable when the elements of conflict outweigh those of cooperation. What exactly happens in this process and how can it be defined under present international conditions?

In an interdependent world like ours, nation-states are becoming increasingly "penetrated" or "permeated"[11] as a result of modern technology and multiple human activities transcending national borders. Such examples may vindicate the conclusion reached by James Rosenau that "traditional boundaries separating the nation-states from the environing international system are becoming increasingly obscured."[12] Conversely, national resurgence is stronger than ever and the thrust of nationalism permeates world politics with a unique force. Never in history have the principles of independence, sovereignty, and noninterference in internal affairs acquired such a powerful appeal. The reason for this state of affairs is quite simple: however penetrated or permeated, the nation-state is still the armor of all small, weak, and poor nations in their struggle against domination or exploitation by the mighty and rich powers. Sovereignty constitutes the last line of defense for the overwhelming majority of nations because as a rule traditional boundaries are commonly violated by the great powers roaming all over the place.

This is not to deny that modern technology and interdependence have somewhat modified the concept of sovereignty. In fact, sovereignty has always had to adapt to historical and technological conditions. Today, also, nation-states are voluntarily adjusting themselves to new circumstances, making decisions with regard to flight corridors and landing rights, radio wave frequencies, television programs, and so on. What nevertheless counts in the final analysis and remains vital to the nation is that its decisions be made *inside* and not dictated or manipulated from outside.

Karl Deutsch's description of sovereignty as an intensive type of autonomy fits my own demonstration perfectly as does the application of his formula: a state is sovereign, looked at from outside, if its decisions cannot be commanded or reversed dependably from its environment; looked at from the inside, it is sovereign if it possesses a stable and coherent decisionmaking machinery within its boundaries. [13] Consequently, I view the essence of supranational integration as *the transfer of decisionmaking power from the nation to a larger entity*.

Let me say from the very outset that this is perhaps the most complex and sensitive social phenomenon, a subject loaded with heavy traditional, historical, institutional, ideational, and psychological charge—i.e., the modern nation. The study of its vital force has led me to the conclusion that to make nations shift their loyalties, expectations, and political activities toward a new and larger center of power would require a very long time during which gaps in development and discrepancies in power among nations would have to be overcome; those nations that have been oppressed, exploited, and underprivileged would have to be given opportunities for the full development and assertion of their economic, cultural, and political potentialities.

Marx's famous thesis to the effect that a socioeconomic system will not pass to a higher historical stage unless it has exhausted its productive potentialities is just as valid with respect to the cultural, creative assets that nations are supposed to renounce in a larger political unit. Indeed, the poor and underdeveloped nations will fail to assert their particular attributes only at the price of feeling dissatisfied and frustrated.

WHAT IS TO BE INTEGRATED?

In dealing with such a complex phenomenon, one should perhaps ask a very simple question: what actually is going to be integrated? Would all the components of nations be incorporated into the new, larger group and if not all, which ones? Would included elements maintain their format and structure. If so, how would the new unit function, make decisions and enforce them?

To answer these questions, we are going to use the analytical model described in Chapter 3.

Natural-Material Basics

To start with, size of territory and population is an extremely important factor in integration for one could easily assume that nations with smaller territories and populations would be reluctant to join with a large nation through fear of being swallowed by the latter. Hence, the asymmetrical structure of projected larger units constitutes a big obstacle to their initiation and realization. Conversely, a symmetrical constellation of nations enhances the prospects for integration.

As for geographic variables, territorial contiguity is probably a prerequisite of integration particularly when the setting allows easy transportation and communication. Thus, while contiguity has been a factor contributing to the success of the European Economic Community, discontiguity—notably, the distance between Britain and Austria or that between Portugal and Scandinavia—seems to have been one of the main reasons why the European Free Trade Association (EFTA) turned into a very loose union. Throughout history, contiguous empires such as tsarist Russia and China have proved considerably more stable than scattered ones like the Spanish and British. However, modern technology and especially modern means of transportation and communication (broadcasting, television, telephone, etc.) have reduced the impact of geography on international politics in general and on integration in particular. Alaska's strong ties with the United States support this point.

Among the natural-material basics, productive forces and other facets of development constitute perhaps the most important factor in integration. Indeed, *homogeneity in development* has proved essential for the success of a large union of nations. All nine members of the European Economic Community are industrialized in the sense that over 50 percent of their labor force is engaged in nonagricultural production and manufactured goods dominate their exports; they are all close in per capita GNP and standard of living. To promote its success, the CMEA has set as a primary objective the evening out of development levels among its members.[14] Therefore, what ultimately counts in supranational integration is a relatively uniform level of economic and technological development. This means that none of the participant countries should be in an economic-technological position to take advantage of the situation, especially if economic superiority is accompanied by military preponderance.

Societal Structure and Forces

Let us now turn to the second layer involved in integration: societal factors. Here we proceed from the assumption that for a nation to be successfully incorporated into a larger unit it must be integrated itself. In other words, a society that is not integrated at the national level can hardly be a stable component of a supranational organization.

This constraint raises the interesting question of whether a nation whose social structure is based on classes with conflicting interests and aims may become a reliable member of a larger union or, to rephrase the question, whether a union based on class societies can succeed.

Amitai Etzioni has identified "low unit-integration" as a condition impeding unification and points to the Congo's falling apart in the early 1960s and the case of Brazil, which during roughly the same period was so overwhelmed by internal problems that few resources and little attention could be devoted to leadership of a prospective regional union.[15] Some writers consider that underdeveloped countries are in general not ready to form larger unions; newly independent states must first succeed in consolidating themselves. Yet national integration is a precondition equally important for highly developed and mature nations embarking upon assimilation.

Recently, a conservative journalist began a description of the Western European scene with "Little England stewing in its class tensions" and then went on to other members of the EEC: "Except for West Germany, all are experiencing economic difficulties and political instability including—in France and Italy—the prospect of Communist participation in government.[16] Clearly, this description does not convey the image of a stable community.

In assessing the role of societal forces, homogeneity of class structure is surely an enhancing factor in initiating a larger union. By class structure I mean not so much the classes that form the nation, as the basic relationship among them, particularly the class that is in power. In certain countries the ruling class is called the establishment; some political scientists use the term power elite. Homogeneity in this respect is indispensable in both the initiation and the process of supranational integration.

However slight the degree of unification (economic or military) the Common Market as well as NATO owe their creation and preservation to the fact that all their member states have a capitalist structure with the bourgeois class on top. Likewise, though of course involving a different class structure, the Warsaw Pact and CMEA are socialist states run by communist parties. Consider, however, that the two German states and the two Koreas cannot be unified because they lack homogeneity of social structure, the two parts in each case having different types of ruling classes. Vietnam could be unified only when the social structure of the North was extended to the South.

Whereas homogeneity of social structure is indispensable in the formation of larger units, homogeneity of political regimes, though important, is not crucial as long as they represent the same basic social structure. NATO, for example, included parliamentary democracies and an authoritarian dictatorship, Portugal, as well as the Greek military dictatorship, until both collapsed. In the Latin American Free Trade Association (LAFTA), military juntas sit around the table with parliamentary leaders whose nations all exhibit similar social structures.

Some degree of political heterogeneity obviously can be tolerated; a large degree, however, may cause disintegration. The British Commonwealth, despite its almost boundless tolerance for diversity, could not encompass both white, racist South Africa and the new black African states once the race issue was made salient, and South Africa was pressured into leaving the Commonwealth.[17]

Although homogeneity of ethnic background, cultural tradition, language, and religion have been deemed essential in the formation of nations, these factors do not carry the same weight in the development of supranational units. Great diversity in cultural tradition and language, for instance, did not preclude the formation of NATO, the EEC, the Warsaw Pact, or the CMEA. (True, there is considerable controversy on this subject: some authors hold that homogeneity in such characteristics must precede all unions;[18] others argue that shared culture is not a prerequisite for unification but rather a requirement to be fulfilled before the process can be advanced.[19] I agree with the latter position.)

The actual relevance of societal factors in the whole process of integration depends largely on their dynamic political action. As an illustration, the Princeton group maintains that privileged social groups (e.g., the Prussian nobility in German unification) have succeeded almost invariably in winning concessions to their interests and views in integration movements.[20] One researcher found that French business leaders who were vitally interested in exports enthusiastically welcomed the EEC, while those who had no export business were less eager.[21]

Big industrialists generally have been the strongest promoters of the EEC, and many of them have merged, managing to acquire control over sizable portions of the EEC market (Belgium's Gewaert with West Germany's Agfa; the Netherlands' Philips and West Germany's Siemens; West Germany's Bleyle and France's Giller; France's Renault and Italy's Alfa Romeo). All told, in 1964 there were about thirty thousand marketing and manufacturing agreements within the Common Market. One notable concession that big business extracted from the economic union was the revocation of anticartel and antitrust legislation; practically no steps were taken to prevent the giant corporations from consummating their mergers and their seizures of market control. Unquestionably, these corporations have been the chief beneficiaries of economic integration.*

Being a matter of politics, integration is understandably viewed by classes and other social groups as a means either of consolidating existing privileges and gaining more power for the ruling classes or of gaining greater social and political equality (of winning additional rights or liberties for the underprivileged, oppressed, and exploited classes).

Surely the primary consideration of nations assessing supranational integration is the size and power of the units joining in the venture. The importance of this factor varies with the scope and character of the planned union. In the case of an economic union, what is important is not the absolute military power or industrial potential of the participants but the relative weight of these features in the specific functional context of the emerging union. For example, France's possession of nuclear weapons is irrelevant in the

---

*The rate of industrial concentration (mergers and absorptions in France, West Germany, and the other four countries increased from an annual average of sixty in the pre-EEC period of 1954-1961 to 150 in the period of 1961-1965 (*Economie et politique* [Paris], nos. 143-144, June-July 1966, p. 174).

context of the European Economic Community, and Belgium and Switzerland were in many respects the equals of Italy and West Germany in the Organization for European Economic Cooperation (OEEC) because of their large capacity to export and import as well as to provide credit.[22] However, when a *political* union is proposed, then absolute military power and the industrial potential of prospective members assume primary significance, and excessive disparities in size and power may prove an insurmountable obstacle. Even when a purely economic union is contemplated, such disparities may be intolerable. Consider, for instance, the suggestion of the Rockefeller Brothers Fund for a Western Hemisphere common market or free trade area to include the United States, Canada, and all twenty Latin American republics.[23] In Lincoln Gordon's view, this proposal is neither desirable nor feasible. It would cut across the developmental aspirations of the industrializing nations of Latin America, nations whose governments differ in many economic policies but agree on the importance of protecting their infant industries from being throttled by massive U.S. competition. Merely to make such a proposal would provoke charges of a new form of economic imperialism from the "Colossus of the North."[24]

Ernst Haas and Philippe Schmitter maintain that under modern conditions economic and political unions are best treated as a continuum. They conceive of integration as involving the gradual politicization of activities initially considered "technical" or "noncontroversial."[25] On this premise the authors predicted that the politicization of the EEC would occur almost automatically.[26]

The facts, however, have shown that such optimism with regard to the rapid politicization of the Common Market was unfounded. This prediction was unfortunately based on a lack of appreciation of the qualitative leap from economic union (actually the EEC is only a customs union: economic policy is still made on a national basis) to political union. Whereas uniformity of industrial development and per capita GNP among Common Market members is a necessary condition it is not sufficient for political integration. The relative, overall national power of each of the nine participants becomes the key factor here. And on that count, there are significant dissimilarities among the nine in both absolute military power and economic potential. France has big power status and atomic weapons and is not prepared to give up either and to join a political union that West Germany, with its superior industrial and financial strength, would dominate.

What has really encouraged political units to overcome such obstacles is external competition. The most serious form of such competition is military threat. A sense of military insecurity, with the consequent felt need for common defense, is currently listed among the factors present in every case in which the desire for federation arose. K. C. Wheare suggested that it is very difficult for federal unity to be preserved, even if it is successfully initiated, without the sense of danger; as illustrations he offered the West Indian Federation, French West Africa, and French Equatorial Africa.[27]

The defense of certain higher legal and/or economic standards has been cited as having helped promote a strong movement toward unity among Austria, Bohemia, and Hungary in the face of a Turkish challenge around 1526.[28] In our own time, the establishment of supranational military organizations has been predicated on the fear of a common threat coupled with ideological considerations: when NATO was created the "peril from the East" was invoked; the Warsaw Pact was established to forestall "aggression on the part of Western imperialism." Conversely, a military alliance formed to counter an enemy will tend to disintegrate as the threat passes (though some defensive alliances do mature into lasting unions).[29]

Thus, a general conclusion may be drawn that regional integration responds to certain common environmental features no matter how elusive or temporary. It is based on certain common needs—often mutual defense against an outside force—felt by all participants. However, while the international setting produces factors favoring integration, they are never sufficient in themselves to explain the rate and intensity of this process.[30]

Contingency Factors

Contingency factors constitute by their very nature a set of highly accidental and loose variables in international relations. They affect in one way or another the initiation, maintenance, and termination of unification. But contingency factors act from outside: they are not part of the phenomenon of integration itself. They do not integrate and are not supposed to. Moreover, they should not be confused with background conditions, which are more or less long-term and somewhat inherent in the process or its initiation. That is, background conditions are part of a causal relationship, whereas contingency factors are not.

Political, economic, and military events may nevertheless accelerate or slow down the unification process. But since such events are unpredictable, it is difficult to establish general rules or laws as to their impact on this process. A political crisis like that which occurred in France in May 1968 undoubtedly had a negative effect on the Common Market, and at that time quite a few analysts were pessimistic about France's future allegiance to the Community. The devaluation of the pound in 1967 seriously diminished Britain's chances of joining the EEC, and the weakening of its currency and the deficit in its balance of payments were used by President de Gaulle for many years as arguments against Britain's admission to the Community. A similar negative impact was recorded in 1969, when the French franc was devalued and the West German mark was revalued.

As for military contingencies, the protracted American aggression in Vietnam has always been considered by the Western European partners as representing a significant shift in U.S. strategic priorities from Europe to Asia and as such detrimental to NATO. The 1956 British-French aggression in Suez was likewise construed by the allies. This is not to say that NATO is a peace-oriented organization, but both cases illustrate the proposition that any military action unilaterally undertaken by a member of a larger union has a negative effect on the cohesion of the latter.

The impact is quite different, of course, when a military action is defensive in character and involves the basic interests of all the participants in a union. Throughout history many alliances have been concluded by nations under the threat of outside aggression.

In summing up the relevance to integration of the three sets of variables—natural-material basics, societal structure and forces, and contingency factors—I must emphasize that the former two may be regarded as the infrastructural layers existing and operating on a national basis, whereas the third is immaterial and ephemeral. Once national frontiers are erased by larger unions, both infrastructural layers are supposed to be absorbed by the new whole; contingency factors will operate at the new level of unification.

What happens to the remaining superstructural sets of variables, state system and leadership, where decisionmaking power and national sovereignty are actually located?

State System and Leadership

None of the various unions discussed thus far has developed a supranational authority superseding the sovereignty of its members. The concept of union, in fact, is often used by sociologists in a rather loose and ambiguous way to cover a great variety of forms of cooperation among nations that retain their individual decision-making powers and sovereignty while entering into common activities and commitments of limited, well-defined scope. Thus, "union" may apply equally well to economic forms of cooperation and/or integration such as the EEC, COMECON, EFTA, and LAFTA; to military alliances such as NATO and the Warsaw Treaty; and to regional organizations such as the OAU, the Scandinavian Community, and the OAS. In other words, the term "union" encompasses all combinations of nations that have established a special link among themselves and might possibly develop in the direction of a political community.

Let us again recall that the shift from a union, or for that matter from a nation, to a supranational unit represents a qualitative change whose essence is the transfer of decisionmaking power to a larger unit. In other words, the crux of the matter is national power.

With regard to integration, the most relevant aspect to be discussed here is the relationship between *state* and *society*. Starting from Hegel's famous distinction between civil society and the state, Engels argued that the state is a product of society at a certain stage of development; once society is cleft into irreconcilable antagonisms between classes with conflicting economic interests, a power apparently standing above society becomes necessary to moderate the conflict and to keep it within the bounds of "order." This power arising out of society but placing itself above it, and increasingly separating itself from it, is the state.[31]

Since the time of Engels a significant change has taken place in the relationship between power and society. I contend that the state in developed countries can no longer be described as a power that places itself above society and increasingly separates itself from it, at least not the state system as it exists today. A clear distinction must now be made between the administrative apparatus, which today consists of millions of men on the state payroll, and the political organs proper (chief executive, government), with their enforcement machinery designed to secure the domination of society by the capitalist class (if necessary through violence).

Indeed, the administrative apparatus now extends far beyond the traditional bureaucracy of the state, encompassing a large variety of economic and cultural enterprises and institutions in which the state is directly or indirectly involved. Modern economy needs many things: coordinated administration of territory, great public works, roads and highways, maritime and air transportation, telecommunications, basic research in science and technology, global projections of future development. Public services and utilities have immensely expanded; public education and health services, including welfare, have reached tremendous dimensions. Defense has become a

Table 2. Average Annual Rate of Growth (percent)

	1938-1947	1947-1956	1956-1965
Employment in the economy as a whole	2.8	1.1	0.9
Employment in the state apparatus	3.5	2.9	2.9

SOURCE: A. Mileikovsky, "The State in Capitalist Society," *Novoye Vremya* (Moscow), No. 41 (October 14, 1970), p. 19.

multibillion dollar business with millions of employees. Only a small part of these activities is still managed by private enterprise; most are performed by the state and financed by its skyrocketing budget.

Indicative of the growing economic and cultural role of the state is the fact that the number of people on state payrolls is increasing at a faster rate than that of the total labor force. The data in Table 2 throw light on this disparity in the West.

A vast and multifarious administrative apparatus has thus become vital to the modern industrial state. The great diversity and complexity of its functions obscure the fact that it is the politically dominant class in each country that avails itself of this complexity to safeguard its rule and keep its hand on the rudder. What is more, the offices of the administration are distributed as prizes and rewards to the faithful servants of the system who subscribe to its ideology.[32]

Nonetheless, the administrative arm of the state no longer stands above society or tends to separate itself from it: it is now an integral part of society—an important point in assessing its "fate" in the process of integration. Whereas the other arm of the state, the political organs empowered to make decisions and enforce them, will necessarily be dismantled upon the transfer of decisionmaking power to a larger unit, the administrative apparatus will persevere and adapt to the conditions of the new community, having a useful purpose to serve in its reconstructed economic and cultural life. In the Third World, the state still has an essential role to play not only as the main instrument of economic organization and modernization but also as the molder of the nation, particularly in Africa and Asia. This is one more reason why the developing nations are not ready for supranational integration. The question of the state and of integration in general in the socialist world must be examined in a different context and perspective; therefore, I deal with this problem separately.

WHO INTEGRATES WHOM?

In a world like ours, with vast power and wealth disparities among nations, it seems a legitimate question to ask whether such unequal partners may successfully form communities larger than the nation and ultimately one world.

According to Etzioni, there are two major ways of forming a new corporate body: (1) a nation more powerful than the other potential members guides the unification process; or (2) many units merge, each contributing a more or less equal part. The power center of the emerging community in the second case would be a genuinely new unit rather than an existing unit subordinating other participants. One might refer to the first system as elitist and to the second as egalitarian unification.[33]

Throughout history, elitist unification (an elegant euphemism for unification through coercion) has been far more common than egalitarian. Thus, Prussia unified Germany through "blood and iron," in Bismarck's harsh phrase. Similarly, the English created the United Kingdom by coercing the Welsh, Scotch, and Irish into union. And the story has been much the same for most empires, federations, and multinational states of the past.

Elitism is sometimes justified on the ground that unification requires the existence of a single "core" unit and that "monoelite unions" are more successful than any other type. This argument, however, makes it necessary to consider the historical context. Thus, despite its coercive techniques, the Roman Empire was successful for about five centuries. Nor was the German union weak or ineffective because of the methods Bismarck used to establish it with Prussia as the center.

Let us, however, take a closer look at these cases. The Romans invaded and occupied vast foreign territories at a time when slavery excluded the majority of the population from the political community. Once it had defeated the slave owners and their armies, a Roman legion could stay in control for a century or so. As for Germany, Prussia unified the Bavarian, Baden, Saxon, and other nationalities, which had already established strong common cultural and economic ties among themselves. In the case of the United Kingdom, distinct ethnic communities were involved in the unification process, and these groups—the Welsh, Scotch, and Northern Irish—are today laying claims to equal status with the core unit, England.

The modern historical context is totally different: nations tend to be rather well integrated; national consciousness and human rights are going strong these days, and "core" units will challenge them only at the risk of failure. Indeed, Egypt tried it with Syria, and the union had a very short life. The Commonwealth, with Britain as the "monoelite" of a loose union, could not survive the epoch of national renaissance in Asia and Africa. The West Indian Federation conceived and initiated by the British as a union of their former Caribbean possessions (with Jamaica as the core) collapsed very quickly. The Jamaicans opposed unification with the less developed islands, and the small islands, although expecting some benefits from federation, feared domination by the larger members. Finally, the core unit was not in a real position of advantage since Britain continued to take her lion's share anyway.

As for Western Europe, there was no such elite unit in the European Coal and Steel Community. Nor can one point to a "core" in the Benelux arrangement. President Kennedy's "Grand Design," essentially an attempt to initiate a larger Atlantic union with the United States as its "core," had the effect, if any, of strengthening the European Economic Community.

The transplantation into the present of a method that sometimes worked in the past is rationalized on the basis of efficiency. Etzioni, for example, expects a monoelite union to be more successful than any multielite pattern for the same reasons that students of corporations have found the monocratic organization the most effective form of administration; that is, when there is only one elite unit, it provides a clear center of policy formation, direction, and responsibility and a locus at which conflicts can be resolved. The monocratic approach is perhaps best illustrated in the following appraisal by Etzioni: "The increased strain in the Communist bloc since the rift between the Soviet Union and China illustrates the decline in directiveness that accompanies a shift from a mono to a dual-elite international system."[34]

The question, however, is whether nations can in fact be run like corporations. If we go as far back as 1943, when the decision was made to disband the Communist International as the center of the movement, we find the historic resolution of the presidium of the Comintern's executive committee stating that

> long before the war it became increasingly clear that, as a result of complications in both the internal and international circumstances of individual countries, the solution of problems of the workers' movements of individual countries on the strength of any sort of international center would meet insuperable obstacles.[35]

In their historical development, the socialist countries have become stronger economically, politically, and socially; the communist and workers' parties of these countries have matured; and their capacity for solving domestic and international problems has grown. A monoelite international system and a rigid course set by that elite are no longer possible. To regard departure from such a lopsided state of affairs as a decline is like saying that children who grow up and become independent from their parents represent a decline.

The crux of the matter is that elitism does not really amount to supranational integration in the sense that this concept must have in our times. For, as Etzioni rightly points out, the difference between a merger of many units on an egalitarian basis and an elitist unification lies in the fact that in the former "the power center of the emerging community is a new unit rather than an existing unit subordinating the others."[36] In other words, elitism boils down to annexation and assimilation of other units by the core. It is the same old thing under a new name.

Unquestionably, coercive power is still a strong component of international politics; the use or threat of military force and economic sanctions are still at large in the international arena, and usually these devices are coupled with propaganda. The point I want to make, however, is that whatever its effectiveness in various international conflicts, coercive power is ineffective in the process of supranational integration.

A heated controversy is going on these days among political scientists and sociologists as to whether coercive power continues to be a meaningful and effective instrument in foreign policy. Some authors, basing their conclusions particularly on the Vietnam war, maintain that coercive power no longer works. Others claim that while it may still work as a short-term policy, it is self-defeating in the long run. In most foreign policy decisions, however, it is precisely the short-term impact that counts.

I would argue that with regard to supranational integration, coercive power does not work even as a short-term policy. To make a nation renounce its identity, with the prospect of losing its own language, territory, economy, and culture with all its symbols deeply entrenched in its conscious, and shift its loyalty, expectations, and political activity toward a new and larger center is possible only on a voluntary basis. This is a crucial decision, a decision of life and death for a nation. It cannot be forced upon a modern nation, peopled by increasingly educated, aware, and sophisticated citizens.

The two cases currently cited to prove the contrary, Santo Domingo in 1965 and Czechoslovakia in 1968, are not very persuasive. In fact, both rather illustrate the thesis that the use of force these days may serve at best only a short-term policy; in the long run it simply defeats its own purpose. In sum, one can safely state that whenever ideological-class reasons are invoked today to justify the use of force against a nation's sovereignty, the inevitable outcome is a loss of ground by the given ideology. And ideology should never be assessed in a short-term perspective.

Therefore, the assumption that force is essential in furthering integration is wrong. Let us suppose, for example, that force had been used against France when President de Gaulle decided to withdraw French units from NATO. Whatever its outcome in military terms, such an action clearly would have critically hurt the unification process in the Atlantic area. Indeed, the use of force in integration generates such intense anger and alienation that unification is inevitably delayed for a long time thereafter.

THE CRUX OF THE MATTER: NATIONAL POWER

Supranational integration represents a new stage in history and as such cannot be studied and conceived in nineteenth-century or even in current twentieth-century terms. What is really new in the transition from many sovereignties to one sovereignty is the transformation of the structure and nature of power itself.

Etzioni, who has looked deeply into the matter, suggests that in highly egalitarian unions power is distributed roughly equally among members so that no one unit has a significant edge over the others while as a group they hold power over any one deviant member. By contrast, a monoelite union represents not a new, emerging unit but rather an existing unit subordinating others and reigning supreme.[37]

However, while telling us that in both cases power rests in the system, Etzioni does not spell out the difference between the two types of power. Whereas in the monoelite union it is actually the national power of the core unit that constitutes the center of decisionmaking and enforcement, in the case of an egalitarian union a new type of power must be created that supersedes the national power of member units and represents the power of the group. This clearly requires that the state power of all members be dismantled, in other words that national power be dissolved.

The validity of this principle is tested every time individual members of the EEC make decisions protecting their national interest that run against Common Market policies and rules. As long as national power is retained by member states, the integration process is reversible. Thus, the supreme challenge of supranational integration is the dissolution of national power.

THE PREDICAMENT OF THE EEC

The EEC is the first modern venture in supranational integration. Still, it is a far cry from the final stage of the process.

The reason why this phenomenon of the future originated in the industrial world seems clear: it is here that technological-interdependence pressure is most acute and at the time of the EEC's initiation the other forces at work in world politics did not pose great obstacles to its drive. On the contrary, they favored it.

Let us consider the explanations given by various authors. A historical study by Deutsch maintains that the most important element in unification movements has been the emergence of a distinctive way of life that necessarily involves a change in many habits of behavior and creates a climate within which political habits of loyalty can more easily be shifted to an entity of larger size. A secondary element he has identified is the presence of some external challenge to the emerging, new way of life. Thus, the common way of life constitutes the major premise for the unification, and the external challenge provides the minor one.[38]

What about integration or amalgamation that is prompted not by the emergence of a distinctive way of life but rather by the preservation of an old, established way of life challenged from both within and without? It seems obvious that this is the kind of situation that informed the formation of the EEC.

A study by Haas lists three sets of background factors for Western European integration: social structure, economic and industrial development, and ideological patterns.[39] However, Etzioni questions the thesis according to which much of the credit for the EEC's success is attributed to background factors (member countries share the same European tradition, have sizable Catholic populations, are at a similar stage of economic development, have a similar civilization and so forth). This homogeneity in background factors, he notes, had existed for many generations but had not prevented fighting among this group of nations. The indicated conclusion is that background conditions alone are not enough; much depends on the way in which they are used—in this case, on the strategy of change employed by those who initiated and supported the EEC. Assuming that background conditions are favorable, it is an effective strategy that makes the difference between success and failure.[40]

Clearly, during its first years, the Common Market enjoyed economic conditions peculiarly favorable to progress toward the goals set by the Rome Treaty. These were years of rapid, uninterrupted economic expansion in Western Europe; they allowed the EEC to create a customs union eliminating tariffs and other barriers to the flow of industrial products among its members and establishing a common external tariff. The EEC succeeded even in unifying agricultural markets, creating a common system of price supports that set target prices, jointly financed by member governments. A second favorable factor was the large, overall surplus in international payments enjoyed by all Common Market countries.

But the economic conditions conducive to economic integration in the early and mid-sixties were at least in part temporary. The May 1968 general strike in France began a turnabout: France's competitive position and balance of payments suddenly worsened, and the resulting disequilibrium within the Common Market coincided with the worldwide deterioration of the international payments system.

In November 1968, France reimposed comprehensive exchange controls, raised border taxes on imports, and even imposed certain temporary import quotas in an attempt to protect its debilitated economy and finances. This policy shift clearly upset the EEC as a whole. With the revaluation of the West German mark in 1969, the Bonn government took similar steps to protect its farmers from the now competitively priced French agricultural products. The result was a debacle for the "green market." Basic assumptions previously unquestioned, such as the irreversibility of economic integration, were rudely shaken. National interests had prevailed. At the EEC summit conference in December 1969, the target dates for various goals, including completion of the stages of the farm program, were set back.

At the end of the sixties a new momentum developed in the EEC. The dimension of U.S. investments in Western Europe and the deep penetration of American corporations in the most advanced branches of Western European industry, particularly electronics and computers, evoked a hue and cry over the "American challenge." Jean-Jacques Servan-Schreiber warned: "if we allow American investments to enter freely under present conditions, we consign European industry—or at least the part that is most scientifically and technologically advanced and on which our future rests—to a subsidiary role, and Europe herself to the position of a satellite."[41]

Even *U.S. News and World Report* (6 February 1967) stressed that American economic penetration was much more important and long-term than the political and military influence exercised by the United States in Europe after the second world war and called this phenomenon "technological colonialism." It was estimated that almost 80 percent of the European computer market was controlled by IBM and other American companies.

A series of measures was then taken by the major EEC members to counteract the American offensive. De Gaulle dropped his objection to Britain's joining the Common Market, and the highly developed British computer industry joined its partners in a coordinated plan to create a more balanced situation in the European computer market.

In 1972, Johan Galtung proposed that the EEC was "a superpower in the making," carefully qualifying this prediction as dependent on the continuation of trends, then prevailing with further extension of membership, and on the deepening of integration. His starting assumption was that the EEC is considerably more than a market: it is a struggle for power, for world power for Western Europe, an effort to turn history backwards to the Eurocentric world of the past but with the addition of modern technology, an effort to overcome the situation in which Europe is *bicentric* with one center in Washington and one in Moscow and *bipolar* with NATO and the Warsaw Pact hostile to each other.[42]

Had power politics been the only—or predominant—force at work in international politics during those years, then surely the power game would have compelled Western Europe to become a true superpower so as to be able to promote its interests and to play a role in world affairs. Since this was not the case and since the economic and technological assets of power have gained ground recently, the EEC has become a center of power even without significant military backing.

Far from charting a continuous course, the history of the EEC has been vacillating lately. In April 1975 the Marjolin Committee told the Common Market that "Europe is no nearer to economic and monetary union than in 1965. In fact, if there has been any movement, it has been backward. National economic and monetary policies have never in 25 years been more discordant, more divergent, than they are today."[43]

In January 1976, the Tindemans Report (prepared by a former Belgian premier who was commissioned at the December 1974 Paris EEC summit meeting to plan the future of the Community) admitted that the recession had weakened the EEC and delayed all target dates for economic, monetary, and political union. The report warned: "If in the face of all these difficulties we go back to policies of national egoism we all face an historic defeat." Tindemans concluded that the EEC needed a strong shot of political will to stay together and suggested as a first priority a united EEC foreign policy.[44]

The Tindemans Report did not make much of a splash and participants in the April 1976 Luxemburg summit meeting could not agree on any of its recommendations. But then President Giscard d'Estaing launched the idea of a "directorate" of the major nations of the Community to streamline the decisionmaking process. One observer noted: "The exclusion of the smaller E.E.C. nations from both Rambouillet and Puerto Rico* despite their vivid protests is best evidence that there already are two classes of nations in the E.E.C., the big and the little."45

Actually, the only item on which the nine members could agree during these years of crisis was the European parliament—more accurately, that it should be elected in the spring of 1978. Agreement was not reached on the powers of the assembly, representation, dual mandates, districting, election day, and other matters.

In brief, the European Economic Community faces the following dilemma. On the one hand, the basic assumption of this union is that the capitalist system will be preserved and even strengthened in the unification process. However, this goal is at present unreachable without the use of state power: state power is essential, particularly at a time when the old capitalist structure is being challenged in Italy and France. On the other hand, the multitude of decisions made by various members of the EEC with the aim of protecting their national interests has persuasively demonstrated that as long as the state power of members rests in the Community, the integration process is reversible. The ultimate success of integration depends on the dissolution of state power. Thus, the EEC is faced with the fundamental internal contradiction of capitalist supranational integration.

THE SOCIALIST NATIONS AND THE CMEA

Differences among socialist nations in size, power, and level of development are great and, therefore, consequential as far as their behavior on the international arena is concerned. There is a vast discrepancy in terms of power between say the giant Soviet Union and tiny Albania, while the per capita national income of the German Democratic Republic or Czechoslovakia is about ten times higher than that of China or Vietnam.

*Two summit meetings attended by the United States, Japan, France, Britain, West Germany, Italy, and Canada.

These differences are reinforced by the fact that socialist nations exist in an international environment whose patterns of behavior are molded by nation-states and the dynamic action and counteraction resulting from differences and gaps among them. As I already pointed out, the radical transformations inside socialist societies have not accordingly changed the international system, and therefore all nations irrespective of their social formation are bound to adapt their international activities to the general motion of the international system. This is why students of international relations find that the foreign policy and external behavior of socialist nations are invariably influenced by their size, power, and development. The Soviet Union and China make full use of their great power status in the Security Council and lay legitimate claims to playing a similar role alongside the major Western powers in the solution of important world issues. Quite a number of socialist nations that are at an underdeveloped or less developed stage (e.g., Cuba, Vietnam, and Romania) have joined the Group of 77 in their battle for a new international economic order, while Yugoslavia is one of the founders of the nonaligned movement and a champion of the Third World cause.

However, one of the contentions of mechanistic determinism is that the ethnic community is determined by the mode of production and from there the conclusion is drawn that the socialist nation represents a different type of nation. In fact, the passage from the capitalist to the socialist mode of production has altered none of the features of the nation—neither its common origin, language, or territory nor its common culture, economic life, or psychological traits. The same observation refutes the other deterministic contention that the social formation defines the nation. Here one may add that the very dynamics of the two concepts are different: whereas the social formation asserts itself by the instauration of the same type of mode of production and social structure wherever victorious, the ethnos expresses itself precisely in that which makes societies with the same type of social formation distinct from each other.

Of course, the transformation of the social structure, economy, and culture has changed somewhat the physiognomy of these nations but not the fundamental characteristics that make each individual nation distinct. For the nations that were at a backward stage of development or were politically dependent, socialism has provided great opportunities for the flourishing of their national potentialities in culture and art; folk music and dances have been promoted with unique force despite the fact that they originate in the past.

In brief, the capitalist nations and the socialist nations are but two hypostases of the same ethnic community: the nation. It logically follows that most of the general rules of integration discussed in this chapter apply equally to the world socialist system.

An objective analysis of this system must proceed by recognizing the historical circumstance that most of the countries in which the socialist revolution triumphed were initially at a low economic level: only Czechoslovakia and the German Democratic Republic were industrialized at the start. A second historical fact is that beginning with the intervention of fourteen capitalist states designed to thwart the Russian Revolution all through Hitler's massive attack upon the Soviet Union, the "capitalist encirclement" has been perceived in Moscow as a permanent external threat. Although the military threat has subsided in recent decades, the feeling still runs strong in the socialist nations that they must be on guard and protect the system particularly since the central capitalist powers still hold a commanding position on the world market and in the international monetary system (which allows them to wage what Gunnar Adler-Karlsson has called "Western economic warfare" [46] against the East).

I make these points because, as previously stated, external threat or competition is an enhancing factor in integration. Indeed, during the cold war, at the peak of the anticommunist strategy of the Western powers, the socialist nations stuck together and responded as a united front. Later on, however, as the class-ideological motive force receded into the background and national resurgence came to permeate world politics, the socialist nations began to promote their own national interests, gradually discovering that these interests do not always coincide with those of their partners. The Sino-Soviet rift occurred and very soon the two great socialist powers had to conclude that their views and aims set them far apart from each other.

The only region within the world socialist system with a geographically focused pattern of interaction among its members that has produced an organized form of cooperation is Eastern Europe, where the Council for Mutual Economic Assistance (CMEA) was created in 1949. Its charter members were Bulgaria, Czechoslovakia, Poland, Romania, Hungary, and the Soviet Union; subsequently, Albania, the German Democratic Republic, and Outer Mongolia joined the CMEA.

Testing the rules of integration in the CMEA case, one realizes that here, too, territorial contiguity has proved a major factor. Still, it was not enough of a catalyst for the formation of a union: homogeneity of social structure and ideology, as the cases of both the EEC and the CMEA confirm, was also needed. Although Finland or Greece certainly qualify for membership in the latter union from a strictly geographical viewpoint, their socioeconomic systems and values excluded them from the CMEA.

The hierarchy of power in Eastern Europe is highly asymmetric, with the Soviet Union possessing an economic and military capability that far exceeds that of any other state in the region. This probably explains why Yugoslavia, though meeting the conditions of territorial contiguity and homogeneity of social structure and ideology, has stayed out of the union, being satisfied with the status of associate member, and why Albania withdrew from the CMEA after the invasion of Czechoslovakia in 1968. Undoubtedly, the Soviet Union is the core unit of the CMEA.

However, what has played a key role in both the initiation and the cohesion of the CMEA is the commonality of interests arising from the fact that all CMEA partners are vitally engaged in the strategic battle of industrialization under adverse international conditions and early experience convinced them that only a joint endeavor could help them overcome these conditions. Hence the remark that the CMEA exhibits the characteristics of a union for development rather than those of a model of socialist integration. To better grasp the meaning of this point, one has to analyze the interaction of the CMEA with Western Europe and the EEC for it is within the European system that the dynamics of the CMEA chiefly originate.

To start with, there is a great discrepancy in the structure of trade, financial potential, and wealth between the two parts of Europe. The share of manufactured goods comprised by Eastern European exports is relatively small (less than 20 percent in the late sixties and early seventies), whereas machinery imported from the West accounts for over 40 percent of the West-East flow. The highly unfavorable structure of trade is compounded by the privileged position of Western currencies in financial transactions; differences in wealth and productivity compel Eastern European countries to protect themselves against the intrusion of Western money by setting forced rates of exchange that make their currency inconvertible.

In general, the Eastern European nations are disadvantaged on international markets: goods manufactured by their infant industries are barely competitive in terms of price and technological sophistication with those of the industrially advanced nations. Moreover, the debts incurred by Eastern European countries with Western banks have reached an all-time high, running into billions of dollars. These data lead inescapably to the conclusion that we are dealing here with a specific pattern of disparity in development. Difficulties in East-West economic relations are in some cases more the result of different levels of development than of differences in socioeconomic systems.[47] Indeed, Europe has *a development gap of its own;* it is a milder version to be sure of the North-South system, but nevertheless one that makes for an important factor in correctly understanding the challenge confronting the CMEA. Therefore, the CMEA provides an internal market that partly absorbs those products of the new industries that could not be sold on the world market except at a loss.

As things now stand, in spite of the tremendous efforts by the Eastern European nations to industrialize and to develop modern economies, their main economic indicators still lag behind those of their Western counterparts. According to W. Leontief's recent U.N. study, their average per capita income in 1970 was $1,564, as against $2,574 in Western Europe.[48]

Under such adverse conditions, the emphasis in the development strategy of Eastern European nations has been on the all-out mobilization of national material and human potential with a regular allocation of a high percentage of the national income for development (Table 3).

According to the prevailing theory in the East, the high rate and efficiency of investment constitute the decisive internal factor of development, which explains why this rate has been kept high over the decades and even raised slightly in recent years. As to efficiency, the recurrent criticism in official documents of Eastern European nations centers on overcentralization, poor management, and lack of incentives, against which various remedies are prescribed.

While the bulk of investments has always gone to heavy industry (machine tools, means of production), viewed doctrinally as the key sector of industrialization, there nevertheless have been situations in which reassessment of the minor role accorded to the consumer sector and agriculture led to a temporary shift in investment distribution, particularly in the mid-fifties (by Malenkov) and more recently in setting the goals of the 1971-1975 plan (Premier Kosygin argued that while heavy industry remains central strategically, it need

Table 3. Development Funds' Share of National Income in CMEA Countries

Country	1960	1970	1974
Bulgaria	27.4%	29.2%	28.5%
Czechoslovakia	17.6	27.0	27.7
German Democratic Republic	18.1	24.0	22.8
Poland	24.2	27.9	37.3
Romania	20.1	29.2	33.7
Hungary	23.1	27.2	29.9
Soviet Union	26.8	29.5	28.0

SOURCE: CMEA Bulletins, Moscow, 1975 and 1976.

not be central in every five-year plan). Soviet economists took up Kosygin's official statement and demonstrated rather persuasively that a lagging agricultural output may negatively affect even the rate of industrial growth, a theory that was conspicuously confirmed in the targets of the 1976–1980, Soviet five-year plan which were set after the poor grain harvest of 1975. However, since Eastern European nations do not have the financial means to sustain both a high rate of industrial growth and modernization of agriculture, the former still is given the highest priority.

The evening out of the level of economic development among the socialist nations, which was considered in the 1971 CMEA document to be "an objective historical process in the development of the world Socialist system" has proved a much longer process than originally envisaged. Czechoslovakia and the German Democratic Republic, which were industrialized thirty years ago, still maintain a substantial lead with respect to all major economic indicators.

In recent years, a more concerted effort toward equalization within the CMEA has followed three courses of action: (1) an accelerated rate of development in the lagging national economies (Romania, Bulgaria) as reflected in their relatively higher rate of investment; (2) the specialization and reorganization of industrial production according to the most favorable conditions existing in individual CMEA countries; and (3) optimization of the interaction among national economies through trade, transfer of technology, and joint financing and building of industrial projects. Table 4 shows the effects of a higher rate of investment on the two least developed CMEA members vis-à-vis the most developed ones.

The projections anticipate that if present rates of development funds are maintained and an optimization of interaction within the CMEA is achieved, the levels of development will be close by 1990. Yet, such optimization is still a desideratum if one looks more carefully into the matter: specialization of industrial production still plays to the advantage of the most developed nations, which enjoy a more diversified range of industrial branches (in 1970, Czechoslovakia's and East Germany's range was twice as diversified as Romania's). This imbalance was clearly reflected in the weight of machine tools in the total exports to CMEA countries in 1971: Czechoslovakia and the German Democratic Republic, 59.8 percent; Poland, 57.4 percent; Hungary, 52.2 percent; and Romania, 29.6 percent (the last had to direct the bulk of its industrial exports to other markets under adverse conditions). Note that in a planned economy, the production of industrial goods is also affected, although not completely regulated, by the external market and that

Table 4. Comparative Economic Indicators of Development for Romania, Bulgaria, Czechoslovakia, and the German Democratic Republic

	Romania	Bulgaria	Czechoslovakia	GDR
1. Development Funds				
1966-1970	30.5%	31.7%	22.0%	21.4%
1971-1973	33.0	25.2	25.7	22.5
2. Growth of National Income				
1966-1970	7.7	8.7	6.9	5.2
1971-1973	11.1	7.8	5.0	5.2
3. Growth of Industrial Production				
1966-1973	16.0	12.2	7.6	7.1
4. Industrial Equipment in Total Exports				
1960	16.7	12.9	45.57	49.0
1973	24.4	38.9	48.7	51.4

SOURCE: CMEA Bulletin, Moscow, 1974 and 1975.

exports of machine tools provide a much higher rate of return than do other commodities.

As for joint industrial ventures, recent data show that the contracts signed with Western corporations greatly outnumber contracts among Eastern European partners. According to a Soviet publication, thirty multilateral agreements have been concluded since 1971 among CMEA countries;[49] whereas in 1974–1975 the Soviet Union alone signed an almost equal number of contracts of cooperation with big firms from West Germany, France, Italy, Austria, Finland, Japan, and the United States (some of which involved billions of dollars).[50] This situation is quite natural from both an economic and a technological viewpoint since the fundamental strategic task of Eastern European nations requires the acquisition of the most modern technology.

Compared to the EEC, the CMEA is much more a state union in which control is entirely in the hands of state power. Whereas the customs union and the commonality of the market play a crucial role in the EEC, integration of CMEA members' economies is achieved and regulated entirely through the coordination of state plans, which reflects the decisive role of the state in running the economy of socialist countries.

This is why Khrushchev's attempt in 1961 to force quick integration in the CMEA took the form of a proposal to create a single planning body for all member nations. This idea was rejected by Romania on the ground that cooperation within the CMEA should be achieved on the basis of the principles of equality, national sovereignty, mutual advantage, and comradely assistance. The planned management of the national economy is one of the funda- mental, essential, and inalienable prerogatives of the sovereignty of each socialist state, and therefore the idea of a single planning body for all CMEA members runs counter to this basic organizing principle.[51]

Truly, Lenin anticipated the tendency of productive forces to develop to the point of "creating a single world economy, regulated by the proletariat of all nations according to a general plan, a tendency that appears quite evidently already in capitalism and which undoubtedly will be developed and fully accomplished in socialism."[52] It is apparent from a careful reading of Lenin's pre- diction that he was locating this problem in the period in which socialism would be victorious all over the world; such is clearly not yet the case. We live in a world in which the nation-state is the fundamental political unit and economies are organized on a national basis in both the capitalist and the socialist world. The best evidence in support of this proposition is provided by the fact that even in the CMEA every new step is the result of bilateral or multilateral agree- ments among member states. What is more, not all socialist nations belong to the CMEA at present, and neither Khrushchev nor the other advocates of quick socialist integration thought of inviting China to join this union.

Nevertheless, one still reads about the "international system of socialist relations of production" described as resulting from the action of "objective economic laws" in relations among socialist countries and therefore assuming distinctive character. The claim is that it is distinctive because these laws function first of all in that part of wider socialist reproduction which is included in international exchange and because their action gives rise to a series of laws typical only of the socialist world economy.[53]

This is a by-product of the deterministic theory (mentioned earlier) that the socialist nation is determined by the socialist mode of production, although a Marxist economist should know better. Socialist relations of production are organized on a national basis and there is no such thing as single international control over the means of production: control is national, too, and the state is the owner and the manager. As for international exchanges of goods, they are carried out not directly but through the state. Export licenses, tariffs, prices, conventions, and accords are all instruments whereby socialist states regulate such exchanges. In some cases, socialist states have made decisions to curtail the exchange of goods with other socialist nations (e.g., the Soviet decision in 1948 on trade with Yugoslavia and that in 1960 concerning economic exchange with China).

To sum up, the CMEA is an economic union based chiefly on the common interest of member states in successfully carrying out their development strategies as a prerequisite to building socialist societies. Therefore, it does not and cannot yet exhibit the characteristics of *socialist integration* which requires the elimination not only of class inequality but also of national inequality.

NOTES

1. Karl W. Deutsch et al., "Political Community and the North Atlantic Area," in *International Political Communities: An Anthology*, ed. Karl W. Deutsch et al. (New York: Doubleday, Anchor, 1966).

2. Ibid., p. 2.

3. Ibid.

4. Ernst Haas, "International Integration," in Deutsch et al., op cit., p. 94.

5. Deutsch et al., op. cit., p. 2.

6. Jean-François Revel, *Los Angeles Times*, 29 March 1970.

7. Nathan Glazer and Daniel Patrick Moynihan, *Beyond the Melting Pot* (Cambridge: MIT Press, 1970). The journals *Commentary* and *Public Interest* are important organs of the neoconservative movement.

8. *Ethnicity: Theory and Experience*, eds. Nathan Glazer and Daniel Patrick Moynihan (Cambridge: Harvard University Press, 1975).

9. Andrew Hacker, "Cutting Classes," *New York Review of Books*, no. 3 (1976).

10. See Charlotte Muret, "The Swiss Pattern for a Federated Europe," in Deutsch et al., op. cit., pp. 149-175.

11. See Wolfram T. Hanrieder, "Compatibility and Consensus," *American Political Science Review* (1967): 971:982.

12. James N. Rosenau, "A Pre-Theory of Foreign Policy," in *Approaches to Comparative and International Politics*, ed. Barry Farrel (Evanston, Ill.: Northwestern University Press, 1966), pp. 63-65.

13. Karl W. Deutsch, "External Influences on the International Behavior of States," in Farrel, ed., op. cit., p. 5.

14. CMEA, "Complex Program for the Deepening and Perfecting of Socialist Cooperation and for the Development of Economic Integration" (Bucharest: Ed. Politica, 1971).

15. Amitai Etzioni, *Political Unification: A Comparative Analysis of Leaders and Forces* (New York: Holt, 1965), p. 17.

16. Joseph Kraft, "Britain on the Brink," *New York Times*, 21 November 1976.

17. Etzioni, op. cit., p. 25.

18. Karl W. Deutsch, cited in ibid., p. 35.

19. Etzioni, op. cit., pp. 35-36.

20. Deutsch et al., op. cit., p. 86.

21. Daniel Lerner, cited in Etzioni, op. cit., p. 287.

22. Ernst Haas and Philippe C. Schmitter, "Economics and Differential Patterns of Political Integration," in Deutsch et al., op. cit., p. 266.

23. *Foreign Economic Policy for the Twentieth Century* (New York: Rockefeller Brothers Fund, 1958).

24. Lincoln Gordon, "Economic Regionalism Reconsidered," in Deutsch et al., op. cit., p. 258.

25. Haas and Schmitter, op. cit., p. 262.

26. Ibid., p. 270.

27. K.C. Wheare, cited in Etzioni, op. cit., p. 30.

28. Deutsch et al., op. cit., p. 14.

29. Etzioni, op. cit., p. 30.

30. Haas, op. cit., p. 102.

31. Friedrich Engels, cited in V.I. Lenin, *State and Revolution* (New York: International Publishers, 1932).

32. See G. William Domhoff, *Who Rules America?* (Englewood Cliffs, N.J.: Prentice-Hall, 1967); idem, *The Bohemian Grove and Other Retreats* (New York: Harper & Row, 1975); Charles H. Anderson, *The Political Economy of Social Class* (Englewood Cliffs, N.J.: Prentice-Hall, 1975); and James Smith, ed., *The Personal Distribution of Income and Wealth* (New York: Columbia University Press, 1974).

33. Amitai Etzioni, "The Epigenesis of Political Communities," in *Social Processes in International Relations: A Reader*, ed. Louis Kreisberg (New York: Wiley, 1968), pp. 449-450.

34. Etzioni, Political Unification, p. 69.

35. Statement by the Presidium of the Communist International (Bucharest: Ed. P.L.P., 1945).

36. Etzioni, op. cit., p. 69.

37. Etzioni, "Epigenesis of Political Communities," p. 451.

38. Deutsch et al., op. cit., p. 52.

39. Haas, op. cit., p. 105.

40. Etzioni, op. cit., pp. 175-195.

41. Jean-Jacques Servan-Schreiber, *The American Challenge* (New York: Atheneum, 1969), p. 26.

42. Johan Galtung, *The European Community: A Superpower in the Making* (Oslo: Universitetsforlaget, 1973).

43. "E.E.C. Writes Off Economic Union," *New York Times*, 23 April 1975.

44. See *International Herald Tribune*, 22 February 1976.

45. James Goldsborough, "Who's in Charge Here," *International Herald Tribune*, 30 June 1976.

46. Gunnar Adler-Karlsson, *Western Economic Warfare, 1947-1967* (Stockholm: Almqvist & Wiksell, 1968).

47. See Gunnar Adler-Karlsson, "Economic and Trade Policies," *International Institute for Peace* (Vienna), no. 3 (1972).

48. W. Leontief, ed. *The Future of the World Economy* (New York: United Nations, 1976).

49. I. Dudinski, "Creative Power of Socialist Internationalism," International Affairs (Moscow), no. 8 (1975).

50. B. Pichugin, "East-West: Economic Cooperation," *International Affairs*, no. 8 (1975): 63-64.

51. Statement of the Romanian Workers' Party, Plenum of the Central Committee of the Romanian Workers' Party, Bucharest, April 1964.

52. V.I. Lenin, *Works* (Bucharest: Ed. Politica, 1956) 31:129.

53. I. Oleinik, "Some Theoretical Problems Regarding the Development of the Two World Systems," Voprosi ekonomiki (Moscow), no. 3 (1969).

6. International Organizations: Cooperation and Conflict

EVER SINCE LIBERAL IDEOLOGY gave to the eighteenth century its lofty message of unlimited evolutionary progress, idealist thinkers and visionaries starting with the French philosopher Condorcet have held forth the promise of a world without war, a world free of power politics, conflicts, and violence. Gradually, this promise turned into the concept of an international organization that would eliminate war and establish the rule of law in the world. Woodrow Wilson, a most eloquent spokesman for this school, hailed the League of Nations as the new instrument of world peace. Two decades later, of course, World War II eclipsed this hope. Rising from the ruins of that devastating war, the United Nations was described by its founders as the international organization that would usher in an era of peace and harmony and, as the Charter proclaimed, save succeeding generations from the scourge of war. In support of this movement, idealist writers offered a theory on the depreciation of power in international politics.

To those who survived the flurry of excitement marking the early days of the United Nations, both the promise and the theory now look exceedingly premature. A number of international military confrontations have occurred over the last thirty years or so involving staunch supporters of the United Nations, among them its founders. Although we have passed the heyday of the cold war, clashes between contending groups of nations, the harsh polemics and rivalries among the great powers, and the insane nuclear race all testify to the fact that we are still far from a warless and harmonious world.

It therefore seems logical to suggest that international organizations are not and cannot be insulated from the world they are supposed to regulate: power relations and conflicts existing world-wide are necessarily reflected in the structure and workings of international organizations. This chapter proposes to focus on the concept of international organizations and on their particular role in promoting cooperation and managing conflict among nations.

My starting premise is that throughout history international organizations have always mirrored the contemporary world power structure. Some authors go even further, maintaining that international organizations are actually initiated by leading powers in order to consolidate their position and to perpetuate long-standing patterns of dependence and domination.

The issue may be approached from the perspective of management of power in international society under the conditions outlined earlier; namely, in the international arena there is no center of authority and power like the state in national society and over the ages the power vacuum has been filled by various schemes of centralization of power designed to perform in the international sphere the order keeping and integrative functions of the state inside society (if possible through international organizations).

Although not exactly an international organization, the Concert of Europe (1812–1914) has been hailed as the "golden age of diplomacy" stretching over a century of "international order and stability."[1] Yet, if one looks more carefully into the matter one discovers that this Golden Age witnessed the imperialist conquest of Africa, Asia, and Latin America that so occupied the European powers overseas that Europe remained peaceful for a while.

The League of Nations, as an international organization endowed with a covenant, an assembly, a council, and a permanent secretariat, constituted a radical departure from previous arrangements: it was a real organization with a legal personality, a structure, and agencies of its own. The League was a step forward in international society. Its membership included more than thirty nations, for the first time providing small countries with an opportunity to participate and to be heard in an international forum. (Indeed, Romanian diplomat Nicolae Titulescu held the presidency of the League for two terms.) Yet, the League allowed the great powers, particularly France and Britain, to control the organization and to exploit it for essentially national ends. By virtue of their special status, the great powers could always—and very often did—frustrate League actions that threatened their vital interests. Thus, the League was totally ineffective in dealing with overt acts of aggression initiated by the foremost European powers. In fact, the Covenant did not specifically outlaw war—this basic constitutional weakness reflected the tone of an epoch in which force was the final arbiter of international conflicts.

The United Nations is in many ways a superior type of international organization. It is much more democratic and universal in membership and much more advanced in its guiding legal principles, reflecting changes for the better in world politics. However, while most of the principles and purposes of the U.N. Charter were drafted with a view to the future, the mechanism provided for in the Charter bears the imprint of the power realities of 1945. The Big Five of the victorious coalition were given a privileged position in the organization's governing structure as permanent members of the Security Council. The claim of the Charter's drafters was that the unanimity principle of the permanent members (the United States, the Soviet Union, Britain, France, and China) would limit the freedom of action of the great powers. Yet, the practical consequence has been that the United Nations is unable to take effective action whenever one of the great powers is directly or indirectly involved in a conflict. Thus, very few military outbreaks have been resolved by U.N. intervention because we live in a small world in which power is ubiquitos. As Stanley Hoffman puts it, "In relations among the Great Powers, decisive for the maintenance of world peace, international organizations stand exposed to perpetual defeat."[2]

Since power relations are never static, the evolution of the United Nations has followed postwar shifts in the worldwide distribution of power. For the first fifteen years, the United States, as the leader of both the Western world and the Latin American nations, controlled more than two-thirds of the votes and could easily prevail. This coincided with the cold war period, in which most analysts subscribed to the bipolar model. By the end of the 1950s a new political factor, the Third World, began to assert itself in the United Nations: the Afro-Asian group became the largest bloc and gradually, with most Latin American nations joining the Third World, the shift in the composition and in the power relations within the United Nations became categorical.

In terms of power relations, then, the United Nations has come a long way—from George Ball's "blunt truth that far more clearly than the League, the U.N. was essentially conceived as a club of great powers"[3] to the present state of affairs in which the great powers complain about the "tyranny of the majority." From a strictly juridical standpoint, power simply does not exist in the United Nations for article 2, paragraph 1, of the Charter solemnly proclaims: "The Organization is based on the principle of the sovereign equality of its members." The same principle is implicit in article 18, which gives each member of the General Assembly one vote (one nation, one vote). To be sure, there are political analysts who take these principles at face value as though world politics were guided by legal criteria and rules. Actually, international power relations are reflected in the United Nations, and the difference between voting patterns in this body and the distribution of power in the world merely points up the gap between juridical principles and power realities. Hence, the theory of the weighted vote, to be adopted in the United Nations, is essentially an attempt to eliminate this gap and to duplicate in the United Nations the power relations prevailing on the international scene.

The contrast between world law and reality may well be the underlying reason why in recent years issues involving the great powers have been increasingly removed from the framework of the United Nations. These countries feel they are in a better position to promote their interests outside a setting that has become too egalitarian and democratic for power politics.

Apparently, the nuclear stalemate outside the United Nations has been compounded by a political stalemate within the organization. On the one hand, to be effective, key U.N. decisions require the agreement of the great powers; on the other, neither the United States or the Soviet Union nor any combination of the major powers can any longer move the United Nations to act against the interests of the developing nations.

A sober evaluation of all pertinent factors will tell us that the United Nations is going through a stage marked by the adaptation of its structure and functioning to the new relationship of forces emerging in the world. The process of adaptation is pushed forward by the new historical actors, most of whom had no say in the drafting of the Charter. However, as any student of history knows, the beneficiaries of the old order will oppose change.

The theory of conflict and conflict resolution grew out of the cold war and has long been dominated by the psychological school in international relations. Kenneth Boulding formulated a theory of conflict as a general social process of which war is a special case. His starting assumption is that in all conflict situations, whether in interpersonal and even interanimal behavior, industrial relations (a euphemism for class struggle, I submit), or international politics, and even animal life, the patterns of behavior display essential similarities, a common element. Boulding has applied the general model of conflict to various special conflict situations to reveal their divergencies from the basic pattern.[4]

From this theoretical basis, Thomas Schelling studied the functions, mechanisms, and strategies of nonverbal communication between parties to violent conflicts and formulated rules for bargaining at the negotiating table and for mixing conflict and cooperation in hostile relationships.[5] Others refined cold war strategy and armed with the mathematical theory of games suggested different ways of exerting pressure on the enemy. A striking illustration of the practice they suggested was the famous "balancing on the brink-of-war" policy advocated in the fifties by John Foster Dulles, then U.S. secretary of state.

Boulding, A. Rapoport, and other theoreticians of the psycho-sociological-pacifist school were at one time concerned that the status of conflict in the international system was such as to lead eventually to catastrophic war. Therefore, they argued that changes were needed in order to divert conflict from violence to debate, to abandon cold war strategic statecraft, and to steer away from the dangerous path of nuclear holocaust. Eventually, the psycho-sociological approach to international conflict became the theoretical core of the American school of peace research.

In general, the psychosociological school, which has been so fertile and creative in microsocial research, has failed to provide a conceptual framework for the analysis of the major phenomena and processes of world politics. Indeed, although one can find psychic reactions in all conflict situations, even in the most subtle ideological debate the simplifying analogy between phenomena that are qualitatively different may not take us very far: individual behavior in a street brawl incited by intoxication or by jealousy is one thing; social reactions in an industrial strike or a revolution or a war are something else. In the first case, it is the individual's psychological motivation that is the determining factor; whereas in a strike, a revolution, or a war, important economic, political, and military considerations override psychological factors. What is more, to the extent that collective psychological reactions manifest themselves, they arise in a context of political and ideological struggle that belongs to the sphere of relations between classes and nations. Thus, many psychologists now criticize the "gross oversimplification" implicit in the assumption that because war involves aggressive behavior on the part of nations, its causes can be explained by examining the determinants of aggressive behavior in individuals; leaders may engage in war for strategic reasons and the population at large for reasons of social conformity.[6]

Apparently, overemphasis on psychological reactions tends to obscure the profound social and economic sources of conflict, particularly class antagonisms and economic inequalities in society, as well as disparities in power or in level of development among nations. I suggest the following points for consideration: (1) social psychology and even individual psychology (when decisionmakers are involved) play an active role in the outbreak of strikes, revolutions, and wars; (2) psychological aspects cannot be dissociated from the social environment in which they originate, nor can they be removed from the basic conflict situations existing in society; and (3) the pattern of international conflict is determined not by psychological reactions, which are temporary in any event, but rather by deep-seated contradictions in the structure of power.

Soviet sociologist D. Yermolenko maintains that the methodology for the study of conflict should start with the analysis of economic, technological, geographical, demographic, social, political, military, ideological, psychological, and other factors and on the basis of such an analysis it should establish the nature and character of the conflict in question, its sources, the stages and levels according to which the danger of escalation increases, and the means of resolving or regulating (in some cases of averting) the conflict.[7]

Quite interestingly, peace research in Europe has parted ways to a considerable degree from its counterpart in the United States. Far from sticking to the narrow behavioral framework of conflict resolution, with its clinical, antitheoretical bias, European researchers have adopted a global perspective and have accepted the starting assumption that the problem of peace is rooted in the very structure of international society and accordingly that dominance and dependence between nations and between groups of nations produce international conflicts. A tentative inventory of such studies will show that they usually focus on six types of international conflict.

1. conflicts generated by the big power game, major strategic rivalries, phases in the arms race, etc.;
2. conflicts arising from marked differences in size, military strength, population, etc., among nations;
3. conflicts arising from long-standing patterns of dependence and domination resulting from gaps in economic and technological development;
4. conflicts between antagonistic socioeconomic systems and ideologies;
5. conflicts caused by social change or civil war that involves foreign powers;
6. conflicts growing out of a sudden bilateral issue in a particular contingency: instant conflicts (e.g., San Salvador- Honduras)

As such studies advance, it becomes increasingly clear that these types of conflict cannot be considered in isolation since they intersect and interact with the result that in most cases the actual conflict is a combination of two or three types.

Digging deeper, one discovers certain relationships among the various types of conflict, their intensity, and frequency. For example, some authors maintain that type 3 conflicts break out more frequently since type 4 conflicts have been kept under control. As Istvan Kende puts it, "Our world is witnessing the coexistence of peaceful coexistence and local wars."[8] Other writers go even further and claim that peaceful coexistence is merely the alternative to warfare among the nuclear powers; conventional, local wars in Africa, Asia, and Latin America may happily continue.

Kende has found that out of ninety-seven wars waged in the twenty-five years since 1945, ninety-three were fought in Asia, Africa, and Latin America; Europe, by contrast, looks like an almost warless zone. Drawing a net distinction between international wars (wars across national frontiers) and intranational wars (civil or class wars), the study follows an interesting comparative approach to the findings of Quincy Wright with regard to wars waged in the period 1900–1941 and reaches the conclusion that the situation has nearly reversed itself: whereas in the past 79% of wars were international, in our time the bulk of wars are fought on the territory of a single country; of the latter, those involving foreign participation are most numerous. Kende concludes that they are in fact a combination of class wars (type 5) and wars of independence (type 3).[9]

While in the early postwar years, ideological conflict was viewed as the predominant cause of war, in recent years Marxist scholars have become increasingly aware that interpreting international politics exclusively in class-ideological terms is not helpful in explaining major political developments. Nations, too, and not only classes play a major role in international politics, and the dynamics of conflicts among nations differ from those of class struggle because nations are great and small, rich or poor, developed or underdeveloped and international disparities, inequalities, and gaps generate types of conflict and cooperation utterly different from those among classes. The point is that social and national motivations intertwine and that their often contradictory interplay is of such a nature that in modern history class conflict alternates with national competition in dominating world affairs. Earlier I labeled this phenomenon the seesaw of class and national motive force in world affairs (see Chapter 2).

At the end of the fifties, with the halting of the revolutionary wave in Europe, the center of social change shifted toward the underdeveloped continents. The West's economic boom and expansion reinforced the conviction that monopoly capitalism had succeeded in controlling its explosive social problems. This basic appraisal produced the switch from the cold war to the development decades, from confrontation to negotiation in East-West relations, from the doctrine of massive retaliation to that of limited war made to order for Third World conditions. Against this background, the nuclear stalemate, the French troop withdrawal from NATO, the Sino-Soviet rift, and national resurgence in the developing nations are all manifestations of a new stage in which the predominant motive force in world politics is national-strategic.

As the new nations began to assert themselves, many Western commentators expounded the thesis that civil wars, coups d'état, and guerrilla and underground movements may well represent the means through which the power structure in the developing nations will be determined in the foreseeable future. In the United Nations the formula was "indirect aggression." The real problems of the Third World nations—economic and cultural backwardness, illiteracy, single-crop agriculture, uneven trade—were played down, while the techniques of the power struggle were dwelt upon excessively. It was not until the sixties that the problem of underdevelopment acquired its real dimension in the United Nations. In parallel, scholarly research work rose to the occasion and began to probe the multiple sources of conflict in the international environment.

Here, one should recall Lenin's three main contradictions built into imperialism: that between capital and work, that between the metropoles and the colonies, and that among the imperialist powers themselves.[10] Over half a century has elapsed since Lenin identified these contradictions, and radical changes have occurred in the international arena, including the appearance of a new type of contradiction, that between capitalism and socialism. Even Lenin's classical thesis that war is inevitable so long as imperialism exists has become questionable under present conditions.[11] The reference, of course, is to world war.

Hence, peace researchers have focused on the historical and structural formation of conflicts in contemporary international society. Dieter Senghaas starts from the premise that the development of capitalism and anticapitalist movements has led to the globalization of international politics and to the emergence of an international society. This society is conceived as an antagonistic totality composed of intracapitalist, West-East, north-south, intra-socialist and intra-Third World conflict spheres and arenas of structural violence at the intersections of international and national conflict formations. Senghaas views the north-south conflict as originating in the relationship between the capitalist metropoles and their peripheries, a relationship that is based on unequal exchange, exploitation, and inequitable division of labor; the ruling groups in the metropoles find support in the privileged strata of the peripheries, acting as their political agents and helping the north-south system work.[12]

In regard to type 3 conflict involving military intervention in the Third World, the following case is relevant. Secretary of State Kissinger stated in a 1975 interview: "I'm not saying there's no circumstance where we would not use force," answering a question about the possibility of a new oil embargo. He indicated that this option might be considered when there was "some actual strangulation of the industrial world" by oil producers. West German finance minister Apel, while maintaining that the West should use "normal weapons" (e.g., reduce oil consumption) to seek oil price stability, nevertheless conceded that the major industrial nations could be driven to military reprisals against oil producers "when they have to fear the destruction of their social wealth."[13]

Robert Tucker went even further. Posing the question, "Is military intervention technically feasible?" he suggested an invasion plan of the Persian Gulf from Kuwait down the Arabian coast to Qatar, which he said accounted for 40 percent of OPEC production and more than 50 percent of its total reserves. When President Sadat of Egypt retorted that the Arabs would blow up their oil wells before allowing them to fall into the hands of invaders, he was saying—pointed out *New York Times* correspondent Drew Middleton—what every military man who has studied this problem knows.[14]

Leaving aside the strictly military facet of the operation, the real question remains what would happen to oil exports and deposits? Obviously, this is the kind of scenario that would spell disaster for world production and supply, making the embargo of 1973 look inconsequential. In general, in the north-south conflict the use of force is both ineffective and counterproductive.

We may now conclude that with the theoretical and methodological tools of analysis that are presently available, it is possible to study in a more scientific way the problem of conflict and war as related to international organizations. Eventually, research should focus on the ways and means of resolving conflicts or averting their violent manifestations. The starting premise here is that methodologically conflict is controlled not by constant attempts to suppress or limit it but by its integration into a strategy in which the parties' initially incompatible goals are absorbed and reconciled in a higher synthesis.

The main theoretical question in this respect is that in international politics conflict and cooperation are not mutually exclusive. To be brief, no politics in the international arena is purely cooperative or exclusively conflictual. The very existence of highly conflicting purposes or interests across states implies, and indeed requires, some degree of cooperation among them. One need simply mention as an illustration of this point the cooperation between the United States and the Soviet Union in drafting the two nuclear treaties on testing and proliferation. And vice versa, even in the closest forms of cooperation between nations there is always an element of conflict, as any student of (more or less integrated) military blocs or economic groupings can easily substantiate. It is the peculiar dialectical relationship between conflict and cooperation in international politics that explains better than anything else the fluctuations in East-West or North-South relations.

Another matter to keep in mind is that peace and conflict are not opposites. The opposite of peace is war, the violent manifestation of conflict. Therefore, conflicts need not become violent; a conflict does not necessarily mean war. There are basic conflicts in international politics that just cannot be solved by force, by war.

Such conceptual clarifications are essential in understanding the means recommended by the U.N. Charter to be used in the settlement of disputes between states or in averting the passage from conflict to war. Article 33 provides that the parties to any dispute likely to endanger international peace should first of all seek a solution by negotiation, inquiry, mediation, conciliation, arbitration, judicial settlement, resort to regional agencies, etc.

Now, what distinguishes negotiation, as the most favored practice, from other peaceful means? I submit that it is the element of bargaining, of give-and-take, that sets negotiation apart. Unfortunately, nations being what they are and conflict being an organic feature of international relations, bargaining too often turns negotiation into a dangerous exercise. As previously mentioned, the cold war strategists developed an arsenal of mathematical equations and games designed to pervert the process of negotiation into a bargaining exercise on the brink of war. The art of applying power to subdue the other party was considered the essence of the bargaining process; calculated risk, deterrence, and balance of terror, were their favorite concepts. Some strategists suggested that rationality in the bargaining process could be taken by the enemy as a sign of weakness and, therefore, irrational behavior was the best way of extracting concessions. A theory of escalation from the first rung—ostensible crisis—to the 44th rung—spasm of insensate war—was formulated as a model of dealing with international conflict.[15]

However, the war in Vietnam eventually turned into a cold shower for the strategists. Schelling now is suggesting that the use of force may have a greater effect on the power that uses it than on the victim,[16] and Boulding concedes that violence against those who are morally dedicated reinforces the legitimacy and commitment of the victim, while it undermines the position of the aggressor.[17]

Having considered theories on conflict, let us now see what practice tells us about the effectiveness and competence of international organizations in coping with their main task: the elimination of violence.

Studies of U.N. involvement in international disputes show that over the 1945–1965 period, from among fifty-five disputes referred to the United Nations, only eighteen (i.e., about 33 percent were settled wholly or in part through U.N. resolution; the rest were settled outside this body or remained unsettled.[18] Another study examined fifty-seven international disputes between 1946 and 1967 and found that in twenty-nine cases (i.e., 51 percent) no U.N. action whatsoever was taken.[19] As for regional organizations such as the OAS, OAU, and the Arab League, their ability to settle disputes has likewise proved very low.[20]

One can hardly avoid the conclusion that present international organizations do not have a significant impact on either the outbreak of international conflicts or the settlement of disputes while hostilities are going on. For one thing, juridical interdiction against the use of force, as provided in the U.N. Charter, has a rather limited effect since in the sphere of international relations there are no tribunals and no police to enforce the law. Second, the moral commitment implicit in the voluntary adherence to the Charter by member states has not constituted any more of a check on violence than legal constraints.

However, the performance of the United Nations in controlling conflict has been fairly good in cases not directly involving the great powers or in emergency situations perceived by the superpowers as heading toward nuclear confrontation. The most successful U.N. device in such situations thus far has been the deployment of peacekeeping forces, as illustrated in the first case (lack of great power involvement) by the Cyprus conflict and in the second (potential nuclear confrontation) by the Middle East.

While in the early years of the United Nations, a military staff committee met regularly, the actual military arrangements foreseen in chapter 7 of the Charter and designed to make the United Nations a peace organization "with teeth" never became a reality. In practice, various forms of peacekeeping functioned until the highly controversial Congo affair. Ever since, the progress of peacekeeping has been pragmatic rather than institutional; both the nature of the action and the creation of the particular force (scope, command, composition, instructions, etc.) have been defined in individual conflicts according to considerations of practical politics, including availability of funds.

In the opinion of Oran Young, the assumption of great power acquiescence in playing a secondary role in peacekeeping operations will no longer hold true in some cases: growing evidence suggests that the superpowers are becoming more and more aware of their overlapping interests in regulating coercive actions.[21] At the same time, increasing pluralism in world politics and new coalitions in the United Nations acting to restrain big power influence are pressuring the General Assembly to upgrade its capabilities in the peacekeeping area. Therefore, theories about peacekeeping range widely from the proposition that a permanent, institutionalized military force be created under the jurisdiction of the Security Council to a more pragmatic approach advocating peacekeeping arrangements appropriate to each incident (this school considers a fixed policy unrealistic under present conditions).

One should keep in mind that peacekeeping purports to control armed hostilities rather than find a solution to the underlying conflict. The tendency has therefore grown in peace research to focus on the causes of conflicts. This tendency has been reinforced by the realization that some forms of violence originate in the very structure of international society[22] and consequently that the elimination of violence presupposes an attack upon its sources.

In this respect, there are writers who maintain that present international organizations are equipped to deal exclusively with direct violence; they are not equipped either legally or functionally to deal with structural or indirect violence, which according to Johan Galtung shows up as unequal power and consequently as unequal life chances.[23] Volker Rittberger argues that since international organization is conceived as an adaptation of the modern state system, it tends to reproduce the basic characteristics of the state system. And since the quasi-feudal structure of the modern state system is the very essence of structural violence in international society, it does not come as a surprise that the elimination of direct (nonstructural) violence has been explicitly made part of the function of international organization.[24]

Actually, the United Nations was not intended to support an attack on the sources of the basic conflict between the rich and poor nations. While the decolonization struggle waged within the main components of the United Nations, particularly the General Assembly, began to be increasingly successful in the early sixties, turning this body from a status quo institution into a growing force for decolonization, the international economic and financial organizations have not displayed the same adaptability. The history of the Special United Nations Fund for Economic Development (SUNFED) is illustrative in this respect. Although the underdeveloped countries have made strenuous efforts to get the U.N. machinery to secure the transfer of capital from the developed nations to them, capital transfer has remained under the control of the developed nations.[25]

Quite a few studies have provided sufficient information to show that the World Bank and the International Monetary Fund (IMF) have had as their foremost goal the stimulation of private capital investment in Third World countries. To achieve this goal, the Bank and the Fund have exerted pressure to make governments change their policies and even encouraged political groups or parties more sympathetic to large-scale private capital investments in their own countries.[26]

Such preferential policies are not hard to explain. At the time of the Bretton Woods and Havana conferences, when such international organizations as the International Bank for Reconstruction and Development (IBRD), the International Monetary Fund (IMF), and the General Agreement on Tariffs and Trade (GATT) spearheaded by the rich industrialized nations, these countries were seeking to regulate international exchange, trade, and finance according to their interests. The gold exchange standard established the supremacy of the dollar in the financial system, while world markets were practically closed to the commodities of the southern continents through tariff and nontariff barriers. The Third World, as we understand it today, simply did not exist then.

The situation has radically changed. The Third World is no longer prepared to accept a marginal status in world affairs and is determined to make full use of all available international machinery. Following the initiative taken by Algeria on behalf of the Group of 77, the sixth special session of the U.N. General Assembly held in April and May 1974 adopted two important resolutions on the establishment of a new international economic order and the program of action required as a basis for building that new order.

Many authors maintain that the establishment of a new international economic order, which has been a major goal of the United Nations ever since spring 1974, entails fundamental changes in the world power structure and its institutional embodiments. They realize, however, that a complete overhaul of the U.N. Charter and existing machinery, much as it may be desirable, is not a realistic proposition. History shows how difficult, if not impossible, it is to codify rules when new relationships of force are emerging.

Therefore, the approaches to this problem vary. The functionalists advocate increasing economic and technical interaction among U.N. member states, assuming that a common policy in these areas transcending national boundaries may have a spillover effect in the political area. James Dougherty argues that since the global system is in transition from bipolarity to multipolarity, the universal actor—the United Nations—might gradually gain utility as a mechanism for modulating an increasingly complex equilibrating process.[27]

Functionalism is conservative in character: it treats institutions as given and unchangeable in essentials; and it proposes remedies so that they may work better rather than devising alternatives to them. This is why an increasing number of Third World analysts oppose functionalism and emphasize the need to democratize the United Nations, to expand control over and participation in its decisions, arguing that far-reaching changes are possible even under the present Charter. This approach prevails in the proposals advanced in 1975 by a group of experts on the structure of the U.N. system.[28]

Change must eventually include the question of the power to make and enforce decisions. Up to now, international organizations have never had power of their own for the simple reason that they were supposed to be run by the major powers of the time. Obviously, this arrangement is no longer workable. At the same time, it is equally obvious that a new international order cannot be established without some kind of an institution or authority to secure its smooth functioning.

However, to be able to plan, make decisions, and enforce them, a world organization working on a truly democratic basis must be empowered by its members so to act. In other words, a transfer of power (gradual to be sure) must take place from the nation-state to the world organization. Whether this historical challenge will be met is one of the central questions of world order.

NOTES

1. E. H. Carr, *Nationalism and After* (New York: Macmillan, 1945), p. 6.

2. Stanley Hoffman, *Organisations internationales et pouvoir politique des états* (Paris: Colin, 1954), p. 412; trans. by Silviu Brucan.

3. George W. Ball, *The Discipline of Power* (Boston: Little, Brown, 1968), p. 17.

4. Kenneth E. Boulding, *Conflict and Defense* (New York: Harper, 1962).

5. Thomas Schelling, *The Strategy of Conflict* (Cambridge: Harvard University Press, 1963).

6. Herbert Kellman, *International Behavior* (New York: Holt, 1965), p. 6.

7. D. Yermolenko, "Sociology and Problems of International Conflict," *International Affairs* (Moscow), no. 8 (1968):47.

8. Istvan Kende, "Twenty Years of Local Wars" (Oslo: International Peace Research Institute, 1969).

9. Ibid.

10. V. I. Lenin, *Imperialism: The Highest Stage of Capitalism* (New York: International Publishers, 1939).

11. Statement of the Conference of Representatives of the Communist and Workers' Parties, Moscow, November 1960.

12. Dieter Senghaas, "Conflict Formations in Contemporary International Society," *Journal of Peace Research* (Oslo), no. 3 (1973).

13. Interview with Henry Kissinger, *Business Week*, 1-7 January 1975; see also *Le Monde*, 25 October 1975.

14. Drew Middleton, "Taking Over Arab Oil Fields Held Possible but Dangerous," *New York Times*, 13 January 1975.

15. Herman Kahn, *On Escalation: Metaphors and Scenarios* (New York: Praeger, 1965).

16. Thomas Schelling, *Arms and Influence* (New Haven: Yale University Press, 1966).

17. Kenneth E. Boulding, "Rebellion and Authority," *Annals of the American Academy of Political and Social Sciences*, November 1970, pp. 184-185.

18. Ernst B. Haas, *Collective Security and the Future International System*, Social Science Foundation and the University of Denver Graduate School of International Studies, Monograph Series in World Affairs, vol. 5, no. 1 (Denver, 1968).

19. M. W. Zacher, "United Nations Involvement in Crises and Wars: Past Patterns and Future Possibilities" (Paper delivered at the Sixty-Sixth Annual Meeting of the American Political Science Association, Los Angeles, 8-12 September, 1970).

20. L. H. Miller, "The Prospects for Order through Regional Security," in *The Future of the International Legal Order*, eds. R. A. Falk and C. E. Black (Princeton: Princeton University Press, 1969), 1:556-594.

21. Oran R. Young, "Trends in International Peacekeeping," in *Dynamics of World Politics*, ed. Linda B. Miller (Englewood Cliffs, N.J.: Prentice-Hall, 1968), p. 243.

22. Johan Galtung, "Violence, Peace, and Peace Research," *Journal of Peace Research*, no. 3 (1969):161-191.

23. Ibid.

24. Volker Rittberger, "International Organization and Violence," *Journal of Peace Research*, no. 3 (1973).

25. J. G. Hadwen and J. Kaufman, *How United Nations Decisions Are Made*, rev. ed. (Leyden: Sijthoff, 1962).

26. Rittberger, op. cit., pp. 221-222.

27. James E. Dougherty, "The Study of the Global System," in *World Politics*, eds. James Rosenau, Kenneth Thompson, and Gavin Boyd (New York: Free Press, 1976), p. 611.

28. "A New U.N. Structure for Global Economic Cooperation," United Nations, New York (1975), E/AC 62/9.

7. Transnational Corporations

THE THEORETICAL CONTROVERSY over the multinational corporations is in full swing—and rightly so. The present analytical framework seems thoroughly inadequate for dealing with a phenomenon of such immense economic and political dimensions.

The importance of these corporations is illustrated by the fact that the value added by each of the ten largest multinationals is greater than $3 billion—a figure larger than the GNP of eighty of the world's nations. In 1971 the total value added by the multinationals reached $500 billion, which accounted for 20 percent of the total world GNP (excluding the socialist nations). In that year the liquid assets of U.S. enterprises alone amounted to $200 billion, or more than twice the total reserves of all central banks and international monetary institutions.[1]

The multinational corporation, which has been the subject of innumerable studies and books, is called by apologists an "instrument of peace,"[2] "part of an economic community on the world level, including East and West, North and South,"[3] "the most important structural event to have occurred in many years and very likely on a par with the Industrial Revolution,"[4] and a feature responsible for "the ultimate entry of the world into an era of international government."[5]

Current projections are that by 1990 six hundred or seven hundred corporations will control most of the business in the non-communist world;[6] present trends could result in an empire of three hundred or four hundred multinationals controlling 60- 70 percent of worldwide industrial output;[7] within a generation between four hundred and five hundred international corporations will own about two-thirds of the fixed assets of the world—the World Corporation;[8] and Howard Perlmutter argues that "since the supergiant firms will be represented in all countries, war will not be possible."[9]

Although the publicity surrounding the multinationals betrays ideological ends rather than scientific concern, this subject is too serious to be left to apologists.

TRANSNATIONALS AND NATION-STATES

Truly multinational corporations—that is, corporations owned and managed relatively equally by several nations—are very rare. Pierre Uri has identified only three such companies whose head office is not dominated by one of the partners. However, these corporations are operated by only two countries.[10]

Raymond Vernon defines "multinational corporation" as a cluster of corporations of different nationalities that are joined together by a parent company through bonds of common ownership, that respond to a common strategy, and that draw on a common pool of financial and human resources.[11] Vernon suggests that three out of every four multinationals are headed by a U.S.-based parent company. In 1970 Soviet economist Manukian assembled a list of such international companies: ninety-six, American; fourteen, British; twelve, French; ten, West German; seven, Swiss; six, Italian; five, Swedish; two, Belgian; two, Japanese; two, Anglo-Dutch; and one, Belgian–West German.[12] (Uri considers only the last three to be multinational.) In light of such considerations the term "transnational" seems more accurately to describe the phenomenon.

As Osvaldo Sunkel put it, "a transnational or supranational capitalistic system is emerging, overlapping national states *de facto* although not yet *de jure*."[13] Indeed, whereas the symbiosis between the state and the monopolies has increased the economic role of the state, the new element in this relationship is the tendency of big monopolies to organize production and distribution on an international basis, transcending the framework of the state system and escaping its control. Again we are faced with a conflictual situation that requires a dialectical approach.

In his criticism of the U.N. report on multinationals,[14] Sunkel rightly pointed out that the report moves indecisively between considering either the state or the multinational corporation as the independent variable because there is no conceptual framework to cover the dynamics of both.[15] On the one hand, the report assumes that the state has the power to set the rules of the game; on the other, the report reveals that governments make available a great variety of subsidies in order to accommodate the multinationals, encouraging their expansion and profit realization. Testimony from

John Blair, chairman of the Senate Subcommittee on Antitrust and Monopoly for thirteen years, confirmed that the oil giants, which enjoyed windfall profits during the energy crisis, enjoyed a unique privilege: "In face of a corporate tax rate of 48 percent, the federal income taxes paid in 1974 by the nineteen largest oil companies amounted to only 7.6 per cent of their income before taxes."[16] Sunkel concluded that neither governments nor multinational corporations seem in actual practice to be independent of each other. And the reason of course is that they are both part of a single system and they have to adapt to each other.[17]

The main theoretical point here is that the symbiosis between the state and the monopolies should not be construed as a complete fusion that effectively eliminates their separate identities. Rather, they constitute a dialectical model whose two parts are both united and opposite, convergent and divergent. The question yet to be examined is which of the two is growing more powerful in this new stage of state monopoly capitalism?

During the 1973 monetary crisis that led to the devaluation of the dollar, some of the speculative activities in Western Europe had been undertaken by subsidiaries of American firms. In 1969, operations carried out by U.S. corporations on the Eurodollar market raised the interest rate on three-month loans to an unprecedented 12 5/8 percent; in 1970, their debts on that market amounted to $13,400 million.[18] Surely, all these developments ran counter to the policies of Washington.

The methods whereby the transnationals evade the sovereignty of states are becoming increasingly sophisticated. Having enterprises in many countries, they often borrow in countries that have low interest rates and transfer loan money to countries with tight credit. By subtle maneuvers, the transnationals annually avoid paying hundreds of millions of dollars in taxes. Even in a country as rich and developed as Canada foreign ownership of major industries has caused the government to lose its ability to control inflation, employment, and rate of economic growth.[19]

Lately, American corporations have shown an obvious concern for their international profile. Whereas in 1965 only 59 out of 3,733 managers of European enterprises under American control were European nationals, since the mid-sixties the latter are constituting almost half of the managerial staffs and in a number of European branches the directors are chiefly European.[20] This situation of course does not mean that basic decisions are left to foreigners. As the *London Observer* ironically asked, Would it matter who is on the board if it were just a rubber stamp, as it could be, for decisions made in Detroit.[21] One American expert noted in this respect that "the *de facto* management of foreign-based affiliates is often different from the *de jure* administration and is invariably subordinated to the parent company's international headquarters whatever its form."22

TRANSNATIONALS AND WORLD POLITICS

As a powerful international actor the transnationals are bound to come into contact with the forces at work in the world-system. To start with, the very fact that transnationals act in a world-system in which the rules of economic and financial relations are set by the capitalist mode of production provides the best explanation for their worldwide expansion and for the efficiency of their decisionmaking power and management capability wherever they operate, including the socialist nations. This is not to say that their expansion can be explained exclusively in terms of the maximum rate of profit. Although profit remains an essential motive force, it alone cannot explain why, for example, transnationals have preferred to invest in highly developed nations, where as a rule their rate of profit is lower than that in the Third World.

In terms of our analytical model, the transnationals may be pointed to as one of the most vivid illustrations of technological-interdependence pressure in the world arena. Indeed, their expansion is attributable to the very character of modern productive forces, which transcend national boundaries. Nevertheless, this expansion does meet with obstacles and restrictions, not to mention conflicts, traceable to the other forces at work in world politics. For one thing, transnationals cannot ignore the realities of the power game in an environment in which the competition over markets and raw materials is very often reinforced by struggle over strategic positions, spheres of influence, and military bases. It is thus not fortuitous that so many American companies have invested primarily in American client states like Taiwan and South Korea, where they have found the ideal open door.

What is more, so long as the instruments of coercion and violence are under the control of national governments, it is on these that transnational corporations must rely whenever the security of their enterprises and operations is in jeopardy. Hence, one finds transnationals clustering around the main centers of power in the capitalist world—the United States, Western Europe, and Japan—and reflecting to varying degrees in their activities the strategic conflicts among these centers. Whereas in the fifties and sixties American companies deeply penetrated European industries and markets, raising the alarm of the "American challenge," a counteroffensive was launched in Western Europe in the early seventies: corporations were encouraged to form oligopolies sufficiently strong to withstand U.S. competition. The merger of West Germany's Agfa with Belgium's Gewaert and Agfa produced a powerful company that employs 30,000 persons and controls enterprises overseas and competes successfully with American-owned Eastman-Kodak, which had dominated the photographic equipment market. Likewise, the merger of Pirelli (Italy) and Dunlop (England) created a giant firm that now ranks third worldwide in rubber tire production. According to the *Survey of Current Business* Western European investments in the United States at the beginning of 1971 almost matched U.S. investments in Western Europe.[23]   At the same time, the Japanese giants are challenging U.S. and Western European companies in automobiles, ships, and electronics.

Apparently, intermonopoly competition parallels the strategic contradictions among the main centers of power; in some instances, national governments intervene in favor of their transnationals. Thus, the United States has repeatedly warned Japan to curtail the dumping of Japanese products on the American market, and in 1977 the EEC threatened Japan with import quotas against its commodities. The latter conflict arose because of Japan's booming trade surplus in 1976: the EEC bluntly stated that it would not tolerate another $4.2 billion deficit with Japan.[24]   In other words, when the chips are down on the world market, the capitalist states hasten to assist their transnationals.

However, the transnationals never return the favor. At a time when Britain and France were pursuing a common strategy against the offensive of American giants, British transnationals were swallowing their French sister enterprises one after the other. In 1972 *Les Informations* complained that not one day goes by without a takeover by Unilever of French food processing plants.[25]

If such is the case in the strong and rich capitalist states, then certainly the tactics of the transnationals in the Third World are much more brutal. Here they come up against national self-assertion, infringing the independence of the newly emerging nations. Massive investments in Africa, Asia, and Latin America have been accompanied by political subversion (e.g., ITT in Chile), bitter confrontations over the right to nationalize, the use of businessmen as intelligence agents, political and economic retaliation by home governments and by host governments, jurisdictional conflicts, and corrupt practices on the part of Lockheed and other companies that bribed political leaders and officials in host countries.[26]

The kind of development fostered by the transnationals in the Third World is not always responsive to social needs, particularly those of the poor. In many cases, the logic of maximum profit makes these corporations gear production to the affluent, who can afford to buy their products. Thus, while acquiring the lion's share of the sources of capital accumulation in the developing nations, the transnationals hinder the economic and social development of the Third World. A large part of repatriated capital—in the form of profits realized by the transnationals—is coming from the developing nations.

Thus, theories that present the transnational corporation as a panacea for contemporary conflicts cannot withstand a sober analysis of facts. In a lucid study, Chadwick Alger concluded that enthusiastic assessments of multinational corporations as agents of peace are based on two fallacies: (1) the assumption that any peaceful cooperation across national boundaries will facilitate the development of a peaceful global community; and (2) the perception that the structure of international activity guarantees that rewards of collaborative ventures will be equitably distributed. Actually, the nations with the greatest military might and the highest GNPs tenaciously cling to their privileges and are unwilling to build equitable structures for collaborative projects. Therefore, rather than promote world peace, the multinationals will likely intensify conflict across the increasingly polarized rich-poor axis, reinforcing this polarization.[27]

My conclusion is that the transnational corporation represents a new stage in the development of the capitalist system. Its features may be summarized in a short list.

1. Transnationals exhibit a higher degree of capital concentration and centralization on an international scale.
2. The surplus value appropriated by the transnationals on foreign markets by the exploitation of foreign labor tends to be higher than that on the domestic market.
3. Transnationals accentuate the cosmopolitan character of capital, increasingly alienating it from the socioeconomic environment of the home and host nation.
4. Transnationals generate an international structure of their own, aiming at the creation of new centers of power.
5. By their ability to transfer production from countries with high wages to those with lower wages, transnationals may blackmail the unions and manipulate strikes.

In response to the last tactic, unions are coordinating their activities on an international scale.[28] In 1972, an international union center was set up in London embracing the entire labor force employed by Dunlop-Pirelli in twelve European countries with a view toward counteracting the machinations of this transnational vis-à-vis the labor market. Thus, the internationalization of capital concentration is bound to produce the internationalization of the class struggle and its strategy.

NOTES

1. *Reshaping the International Order*, Jan Tinbergen, coordinator (New York: Dutton, 1976), p. 274.
2. Neil Jacoby, "The Multinational Corporation," *Center Magazine*, May 1970.
3. Howard Perlmutter, "Super-Giant Firms in the Future," *Wharton Quarterly*, Winter 1968, p. 14.
4. Judd Polk, "Economic Implications of the Multinational Corporation," in *Multinational Corporation* (Washington, D.C.: Department of State, Office of External Research, February 1969), p. 18.
5. Roy Blough, *International Business: Environment and Adaptation* (New York: McGraw-Hill, 1966).
6. George Steiner and Warren Cannon, *Multinational Corporate Planning* (New York: Macmillan, 1966), p. 4.
7. Stephen Hymer, cited by Peter Evans, "National Autonomy and Economic Development," *International Organization*, no. 3 (Summer 1971), p. 676.
8. A. Barber, "Emerging New Power: The World Corporation," *War-Peace Report*, October 1968.
9. Perlmutter, op. cit., p. 8.
10. Pierre Uri, "Multinational Corporation and European Integration," *Interplay*, November 1968.
11. Raymond Vernon, "International Business and National Economic Goals," *International Organization*, Summer 1971.
12. *Mirovaia ekonomika i mezhdunarodniyie otnosheniya*, no. 9 (1970), p. 143.
13. Osvaldo Sunkel, "On the UN Report on Multinational Corporations in World Development," *Pacific Community*, July 1974.
14. United Nations, *Multinational Corporations in World Development* (New York: United Nations, 1973).
15. Sunkel, op. cit.
16. John M. Blair, *The Control of Oil* (New York: Pantheon, 1976).
17. Sunkel, op. cit.
18. *Banker's Magazine* (London), February 1971, pp. 65-67.
19. U.S., Congress, Senate, Subcommittee on Foreign Economic Policy, *A Foreign Economic Policy in the 1970s*, 91st Cong., 2d sess., 1970, pp. 913-914.

20. *Time*, 29 December 1967, p. 42.

21. *Observer* (London), 21 March 1971, p. 15.

22. E. J. Kolde, *International Business Enterprise* (Englewood Cliffs, N.J.: Prentice-Hall, 1968), p. 25.

23. *Survey of Current Business*, October 1971.

24. "Japanese Fearful about Exports' Outlook," *International Herald Tribune*, 2 March 1977.

25. *Les Informations*, Paris, July 1972.

26. Tinbergen, op. cit., p. 275.

27. Chadwick Alger, "The Multinational Corporation and the Future International System," *Annals of the American Academy of Political and Social Science*, September 1972.

28. See Ilie Serbanescu, "International Monopolies under Contemporary Capitalism" (Ph.D. diss., Academy of Economics, Bucharest, September 1976).

8. The Future of International Relations

IT IS NOT FORTUITOUS that in recent decades political forecasting and future world modeling have preoccupied research institutes all over the world and governments have been actively commissioning future studies and prognoses. Under the conditions created by the technological revolution, speed of communication and information dissemination tends by itself to accelerate the course of political events. Consequently, decisions made today must necessarily be conceived in terms of tomorrow. Changes in international politics are sometimes so rapid that decisions made exclusively on the basis of imminent contingencies may appear obsolete at the time of their announcement.

However, world politics is a phenomenon so complex that one can hardly manage all the factors that make it work. What is more, in a world that is quickly changing, the priority of factors or problems is equally volatile. With key problems coming to the fore on a worldwide scale, the early seventies brought the threat of destruction to our environment; in but a couple of years this concern was minimized because of the energy crisis and the alarm over the scarcity of resources. Widely acclaimed books that daringly sketched the year 2000 were outdated in only four or five years because they omitted both the energy crisis and scarcity of resources.

The blunt truth is that futurology is a newcomer to the social sciences, and given the state of the art the forecasting of international relations has very little scientific ground to stand on. Though an emerging science, futurology is highly specialized. In various areas—science, technology, economy, culture—short- and long-term projections have been advanced, each providing but incomplete images of future human activities. Forecasting in international rela-

137

tions is a much more difficult exercise because it involves the most complex network of social relationships. Therefore, the researcher must bring together all these incomplete images into a single whole, the global system, identify the major forces that make the world-system work, the trends these forces generate, and eventually the direction in which they are going to move things in the foreseeable future.

Karl Marx cautioned that such future-oriented research should focus on the general direction of social evolution and avoid predicting specific events or sociopolitical developments, which are highly susceptible to accidental factors. Indeed, whenever Marx himself or his disciples departed from this guiding principle their predictions proved to be wide of the mark. Twenty-five years after the publication of the *Communist Manifesto*, Marx and Engels pointed out in the preface to the German edition of 1872 that although "the general principles laid down in this Manifesto are, on the whole, as correct today as ever" the revolutionary program proposed at the end of section 2 had in some details become "antiquated" and owing to unforeseen events and sociopolitical developments that program "would in many respects be very differently worded today."[1]

THE ULTIMATE TASK IN FORECASTING

In recent years, quite a few future world models have been offered to the public and widely discussed in seminars and scholarly journals. It is therefore appropriate to examine their approaches, methods, and implications.

In *The Year 2000* Herman Kahn and Anthony Wiener predicted that the age of electronics, computers, automation, cybernetics, and data processing will make the technology of the 1940s and 1950s look like Model-T technology at the end of this century.[2] Nevertheless, they indicated that neither the social system nor the world power structure will be affected by these fantastic technological transformations. The business civilization will be going strong in the year 2000: "While businessmen will probably continue to be deeply occupied with their affairs, the issues of finance, investments, production, sales and distribution that have been so long dominant concerns of so many Americans and Europeans will very likely dwindle in interest."[3] In other words, business without headaches.

Kahn predicted that the two superpowers will still dominate international relations in the year 2000, followed by Japan, West

Germany, France, China, and Britain.[4] Thus, the temptation to project into the future what one actually desires in the present has proved irresistible. Kahn's world of the year 2000 is the present world, only more so.

In his introduction to *Between Two Ages*, Zbigniew Brzezinski described the industrially advanced countries as "entering an age in which technology and especially electronics—hence my neologism technetronic—are increasingly becoming the principal determinants of social change, altering the mores, the social structure, the values, and the global outlook of society."[5] Again, the technetronic revolution is not paralleled by change in the social or international structure. We are assured that the future community of developed nations "would not sweep aside United States- Soviet nuclear rivalry which would remain the axis of world military might."[6]

Even the doomsday projections of the Forrester-Meadows world model reflect the assumption that while all other elements are bound for disaster, the so-called population-capital system (read capitalism) will remain intact (see Chapter 4).

Hence, as one looks deeper into the matter one finds that in these projections, the tactical admission of change is always subordinated to the strategic aim of saving the system. These predictions are all very long on *technological change* but very short on *social change*. However, the world is a system; changes in one element produce changes in the other elements and as a result the whole ensemble undergoes change, as Marxism has always contended. Indeed, Marx was the first social thinker to combine the economic base with the social and political structure into a whole, the social system, and to reveal the mutual relationships among its components.

The ultimate task of the researcher of the future was clearly specified by Marx, who emphasized that the positive understanding of present reality also includes the comprehension of its negation and of its necessary substitution by a superior form. Modern sociohistorical categories—classes, nations, states, power—are bound to disappear in a distant future, and the fact that they display unusual vigor in contemporary society (both Eastern and Western) may be attributed to the dialectical finding that social categories perish as a result of their overdevelopment. Trotsky used to compare this phenomenon with a gas lamp whose flame suddenly flares up before dying out. Indeed, world history abounds in examples of this process: the Roman empire began to disintegrate as it reached its apex of power, and it took less than twenty years for the vast British colonial system, covering one-third of the globe, to crumble.

Hence, it seems natural that the old class holding power should find it hard to perform this dialectical task. Never in history has a ruling class accepted the negation of its power and the logical conclusion—termination of that power.

In the Eastern nations, where the old classes are no longer in power, economic planning (which was and remains the greatest asset of the developing socialist societies) has taken on a long-term dimension. However, very few attempts thus far have been made to forecast international relations and no world model for the year 2000 has been worked out in the Soviet Union, China, or any other socialist country even though this is now an important issue in the ideological confrontation. Why this lack?

The most comprehensive study in the East with regard to the impact of the scientific-technological revolution on society and the world is *Civilization at the Crossroads*, produced by an inter-disciplinary group of scholars coordinated by Radovan Richta.[7] One of the relevant findings of this study was that since industrialization historically belongs to the capitalist stage, the construction of a modern industry may constitute at best the premise of a socialist society rather than a goal. The socialist society must create a civilization of its own surpassing the limits of the industrial system. Richta argues that while the scientific-technological revolution is in its initial stages the capitalist base can allow it relatively free movement; once the revolution becomes full-scale that base will prove too narrow at crucial points and collisions and conflicts—ultimately catastrophe—will occur. The new socialist and communist relations of production will actually assert their potentialities only when industrialization will be achieved and the technological revolution will find proper conditions for its full-scale development in socialist societies.[8]

Obviously, present socialist societies are still grappling with the task of industrialization, their rapid tempo of economic growth notwithstanding. This is the fundamental historical and ideological handicap that explains the scientific paradox of the East: the availability of the most powerful theoretical instrument for social prediction accompanied by poor performance in its actual use. I am aware of the diverse explanations for the state of the social sciences in the East—dogmatism, the crippling effect of the Stalinist terror, thought control, and so on. Each one of course has played a part and not a minor one,* but I think that the historical handicap is para-

---

*In his famous work *The Ascent of Man*, Jacob Bronowski noted that the intellectual repression undertaken by the Catholic church and the Inquisition in Italy and Spain reached such heights that it caused the locus of scientific research and thought to shift from Italy to Northern Europe.

mount. In the final analysis, it accounts (at least partially) for the preceding factors.

THEORETICAL MODEL FOR FUTURE WORLDS

In the World Order Models Project[9] each author was asked to start from a diagnosis of the contemporary world order, make prognostications based on that diagnosis, state his preferred future world order, and advance coherent and viable strategies of transition that could bring that future into being. All the participants agreed that humanity faces four major problems (war, poverty, social injustice, and environmental decay). Consequently, their models were intended to come to grips with these problems according to a set of values. Briefly, this approach was normative in the sense that the world was viewed as it should be not as it is.

My approach to world modeling is different. My starting premise is that the specific task of forecasting in the realm of international relations is to study the future evolution of nation-states and international and transnational organizations and systems and eventually the interaction among all these within the world-system. Since we will be dealing with large social aggregations with different degrees of integration and high levels of systemicity, I propose to focus on the two basic types of social relations—namely, classes and ethnic communities—and to see how in the future they will develop their dialectical relationship under the pressure of modern production and technology.

The classical Marxist paradigm for social forecasting is based on two fundamental contradictions: the economic one between productive forces and productive relations and the social contradiction this generates between property classes and exploited ones, turning the class struggle into the motor of history. This paradigm is adequate for the study of the national system. In order to study the world-system, I have added a third element, the contradiction among nations, which is of a different nature from class struggle and very often comes into conflict with the logic of class struggle.

In a study of prospective international relations[10] the French Marxists Alexandre Faire and Jean-Paul Sebord tackled the question of the motor of history and concluded that among the three answers provided by Marxist tradition (technological change, economy, and class struggle) the last is the most modern, synthetic, and appropriate for the study of international relations. Their argument is highly persuasive: class struggles properly emphasize the intervention of man and the role of the masses in history; class struggles adequately reflect the diversity of social transformations and political conflicts; they synthesize the contradictions within the socioeconomic structures in which technological innovations play a definite part. In short, class struggle is the very object of historical materialism.[11]

Figure 2.   Research Design for the Forecasting of Future Worlds

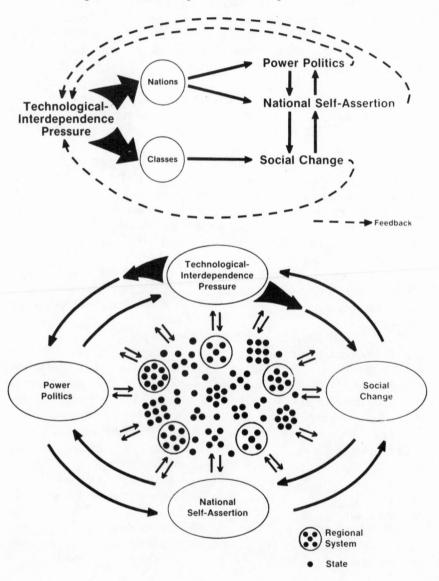

Nonetheless, I cannot agree with Faire and Sebord's proposition that "within the framework of international relations, as in the political struggle inside a country, it is the social classes that confront each other" [12] and with their mechanical extension of class struggle into the international arena. Here the two spheres of politics—domestic and international—are viewed as a continuum and the fact that nations behave according to their size, power, level of development, and wealth is totally neglected. Curiously, in their analysis Faire and Sebord do take into account the special game of politics in which the great powers are involved and they even go so far as to claim that in U.S.-Soviet relations, resting on contradictions and unity, unity is dominant. [13] Yet, they do not draw the proper theoretical conclusion from such a situation, which can hardly be explained in terms of classes and class struggle. In international politics, nations have a drive of their own that cannot be identified with the internal movement of a society.

The theoretical model of my projection into the future of the world consequently is built on the assumption that the pressure of modern technology acts upon relations among nations in terms of power politics and its response, national self-assertion, and in terms of class relations, ultimately producing social change (see Figure 2). The pressure of modern technology is the main driving force toward a smaller world. Yet, social cleavages inside societies as well as international rivalries or differences place formidable obstacles in the path of integration. Accordingly, we may expect the process of integration to be marked by progress and regress, to proceed in stages, and only in the very distant future (probably the late twenty-first century) to encompass all nations. I maintain that geographical and ecological factors will cause integration to occur first on a regional basis.

THE NEXT STAGE: REGIONAL SYSTEMS

What are the regions of the world in which integration is most likely to be initiated and successfully achieved? *World Politics* [14] focuses on seven regional systems: Western Europe, Eastern Europe, the Middle East, South Asia, East Asia, Latin America, and Africa. The authors point out that although these regions differ greatly in terms of geographical configurations, institutional developments, internal cohesion, vulnerability to foreign intrusion, economic viability, and historical traditions, the analyses of these seven have in common a concern for the way in which such variables shape the intensity and direction of regional politics.

Mihajlo Mesarovic and Eduard Pestel have divided the world into ten regions: North America, Western Europe, Japan, Australia and other developed nations with market economies, Eastern Europe, including the Soviet Union, Latin America, North Africa and the Middle East, Tropical Africa, South Asia, and China. The division was made according to traditions, history, and life-style, development level, sociopolitical structure, and similarity of problems that confront these areas.[15] In a more recent study coordinated by Wassily Leontief, the world was divided into fifteen regions according to geography and economic variables.[16] This breakdown has proved to be the most controversial. Eastern Europe is listed in the developed world; Portugal and Spain are put in the same category as Cyprus, Turkey, and Yugoslavia; while Gabon and Nigeria are classified with Iran, Iraq, and Kuwait as oil producers. One can hardly imagine future regional units effectively integrated on such bases. The lack of an adequate conceptual framework is too obvious in this case.

THE 1980s

In a short-term overview of regional developments, let us proceed from the proposition that territorial contiguity encourages integration although it alone is insufficient to effect such change: homogeneity of social structure and ideology is the missing element (e.g., NATO, the EEC, the Warsaw Treaty, and the CMEA). Therefore, let us project the process of integration in the context of the international subsystems exhibiting these features, particularly the so-called three worlds, which should be placed in our model on an intermediate level between the national systems and the world-system. For the sake of analytical clarity I shall first consider each of these worlds separately and then discuss how they intersect and interact.

After years of financial disruptions, recession, and worldwide inflation, the *first world* began to gain strength in 1976, particularly the United States, West Germany, and Japan. The OECD scenario for 1980 sets the targets listed in Table 5.

This scenario, which is half prediction and half guideline, calls upon the twenty-four nations of OECD to grow at an average rate of around 5½ percent annually. A thorough examination of the data points to the conclusion that even if the prescribed targets were attained, inflation for most nations would still be higher at the end

Table 5. The OECD Scenario for 1980

COUNTRY	INFLATION		POTENTIAL UNEMPLOYMENT		GROWTH OF OUTPUT (PER YEAR)
	1975-1976	1976-1980	1975	1980	
Canada	8¾%	5½%	7½%	4½%	6%
United States	5¼	4½	9½	5½	5¾
Japan	6½	6	3½	2-2½	7
France	11	6	4½	3-3½	6
West Germany	3½	4	5	1½-2	5
Italy	17½	7	5½	5-5½	4½
United Kingdom	16¼	6	5	4	3½

SOURCE: Adapted from the *London Times*, 28 July 1976.

of the decade than it was in the sixties and unemployment even more so. Hence the call particularly for the United States to increase its rate of growth, which of course may result in a higher rate of inflation. The novelty, however, is that this scenario is the first attempt to plan the economic development of the industrialized world as a whole. Only a decade ago, this task would have been considered both heretical and unrealistic in the West. The present economic crisis has substantially enhanced the economic role of the state not only internally but also externally, and one can safely predict that the 1980s will be marked by a general politicization of world economics. Even in the United States, where the law of the market and free enterprise are articles of faith, Brzezinski now accepts that "issues heretofore handled either by the private sector or through private-governmental negotiations, largely on the basis of business criteria, are tending to become injected with political content. The effect is to reinforce and in some cases to make dominant the role of political motives and of political criteria in international economics."[17]

The main regional unit taking shape within the industrial world is Western Europe, with the nine members of the EEC constituting its core and exerting an increasingly strong attraction on other European nations with manifest affinities in economic development, social structure, and ideology, especially Spain and Portugal. As for Turkey and Greece, the development gap is compounded by territorial discontinuity, making for an artificial linkage with the West.

Apparently, the commonality of interests fostering unification is too often obstructed either by differences in power giving rise to projects for directorates (e.g., Franco-German) or by West Germany's fear that Britain's protracted financial predicament and Italy's *bancarotta* may ultimately pull down all nine members. The truth is that while the Common Market fared well during the sixties, recent developments are tending to reverse this trend and to encourage each member to take care primarily of its own affairs.

The really new political development of the 1980s in Western Europe may come from a variable that seemed dormant, namely, social change. At a time when economic turmoil and high unemployment prevail, large sections of the population become disenchanted with the system, join the class struggle, and eagerly await change. Whether the political forces of the Left will be able to unite and turn these conditions into a real change of guard is still an open question. In Italy, the Communist party has gained a powerful position in Parliament and in the big cities, while in France, the United Left (Socialists and Communists) may win the 1978 general election. The challenge is formidable and without precedent: Italy, or perhaps France, may be the first crack in the developed world—the core of the international system. Of course, considerable opposition is being mustered. Secretary of State Kissinger bluntly described Eurocommunism as a threat to NATO and Chancellor Schmidt threatened to withhold credits that Italy badly needed. Under such conditions, in a regional system dominated by NATO and the EEC the strategy of revolution must necessarily differ from all previous strategies, as seen in the new approach of Eurocommunism. The main problem for Western European communists is not accession to power, which will be easy, but consolidation of power, which will be difficult in a regional environment wherein international capital is capable of devastating the Italian or the French economy and currency (witness the example of Chile). The logical conclusion is that in Western Europe conditions for a successful revolution must be ripe not only internally but also externally; the forces of change must advance on a broad front (perhaps along the Mediterranean coast from Italy and France to Spain and Portugal). In Northern Europe, we may see a shift to the right, which will generate a new type of conflict within NATO and the EEC.[18]

The *third world*, though emerging later on the international scene, must be examined in relation to the industrial world. While in the early seventies, the poor and underprivileged nations of Africa, Asia, and Latin America managed to organize themselves as a new political factor (the Group of 77) and to call for a change in the international economic order, the eighties will probably see the historical interplay between cohesive and divisive forces, partly manipulated by outside powers.

Indeed, homogeneity is alien to the Third World, and the diversity of its hundred or so members is immense not only in natural-material basics and social structure but also in culture and historical stage. Nevertheless, it is a solid assumption that in the 1980s regional organizations will play an increasing role both economically (intra-continental trade, for example) and politically in promoting the common interests of this world.

National integration is a precondition for any form of larger union and therefore a primary task of the new independent states is their own consolidation as nations. In Africa, the new states have yet to overcome tribal factionalism; whereas in Latin America, where the rich differ from the poor in religion (Catholic versus non-Christian) and in racial or ethnic background (whites versus Indians, e.g.), the degree to which society can be integrated is low. Ulster and Lebanon are dramatic examples of the deep cleavage resulting from social antagonisms coinciding with religious or racial conflicts. One thing is clear: so long as Brazil and Nigeria, the largest countries on their continents, do not overcome internal dissensions, they will be unable to serve as centers of power and play a major role in their regional unions.

In post-Vietnam Asia, marked asymmetries in power and development, not to mention culture and religion, will keep nations apart for a while. Regional unification appears a distant possibility in Asia, where foreign forces obstruct this process. The United States, the Soviet Union, China, and Japan make for a four-sided balance and an intricate power game in Southeast Asia and the Pacific. There can be no easy-to-read East-West scoreboard for victories and losses of positions so long as Sino-Soviet rivalry exists. Thus, none of the four powers listed above will be permitted by the others to act as the core of a geographically organized regional unit in Asia, where territorial contiguity alone is insufficient to produce integration.

In Indochina, postwar rebuilding is a task so formidable that there is very little energy left in Vietnam, Laos, or Cambodia for vigorous external initiatives. Nations caught in the middle, like the Philippines, Malaysia, and Thailand, are discovering that with multiple centers of power in the area there is a better chance for the poor nations to promote their own interests.

Illustrating the contradictory evolution to be expected in the Third World are the cases of a number of African countries (Tanzania, Mozambique, Angola, Guinea, and Ethiopia) taking a non-capitalist path of development. A lucid assessment that applies to all these countries was made by President Nyerere at the tenth anniversary of the Tanzanian experiment: "Tanzania is neither socialist nor selfreliant and the goal of making it so is not even in sight."[19] This goal may not be realizable in the 1980s but it nevertheless points out aims that will become increasingly important in the future of Africa and most probably constitute the focus of a regional union.

A different sort of regional arrangement is taking shape in the Middle East, where the new Arab Authority (set up chiefly with Saudi and Kuwaiti petrodollars) has embarked on an ambitious project to turn Sudan into the breadbasket of the Arab world. This combination of conservative Arab wealth and Western know-how (and money) has contradictory aims: on the one hand, to provide an alternative model to the socialist one, swinging Sudan and other Arab states back to the West; and on the other, to free the Arab world from its dependence on food exports and by extension from a possible blackmail by oil consuming nations. By 1985, Sudan is expected to provide 42 percent of the total Arab vegetable needs, 58% of its grain, and 20 percent of its sugar.[20]

In general, the logic of sociopolitical development in the 1980s will sharpen both the conflict with the industrial nations and the domestic antagonisms within developing societies. Briefly, national self-assertion will combine with social change in shaping political developments in the Third World.

The *second world* will go its own way although not as insulated from worldwide economic disruptions as it once was. While the ambitious targets of the five-year plans were generally attained in 1971-1975, most European socialist nations ran balance of payments deficits with the West in 1975 and 1976.

All the centrally planned nations, whether Bulgaria or China or Cuba, will continue stubbornly to follow their strategies of development based on the all-out mobilization of material and human resources, allocating a high percentage of their national incomes for development while keeping consumption comparatively low. Apparently, from now on China will adhere to the policy line set by the late Chou En-lai at the party congress, which seeks to turn China into a modern industrial power by the end of this century.

The only region within the world socialist system with a geographically focused pattern of interaction among its members, resulting in an organized form of cooperation, is Eastern Europe—with its Council for Mutual Economic Assistance. While all CMEA members have a common sense of identity in terms of political ideology and socioeconomic organization, they differ in terms of economic development, with Czechoslovakia and East Germany maintaining a substantial lead; moreover, the hierarchy of power is highly asymmetric, with the Soviet Union possessing a political capability exceeding by far that of any other state in the region. Therefore, the common cause of industrialization emerges as the key factor in this regional economic union with the proclaimed aim of evening out the levels of development among its members by 1990. Table 6 shows this policy at work.

Table 6. Eastern Europe: Development Plans, 1976-1980

COUNTRY	GROWTH OF NATIONAL INCOME	GROWTH OF INDUSTRIAL PRODUCTION	DEVELOPMENT FUND'S SHARE OF NATIONAL INCOME
Romania	10.0-11.0%	10.2-11.2% (14)*	33.0-34.0%
Bulgaria	7.0- 8.4	9.2 (10)	28.0
Poland	7.0- 7.2	8.2- 8.5 (11)	33.4
Hungary	5.4- 5.7	6.0 (6.8)	25.0-27.0
Czechoslovakia	4.9- 5.25	5.7- 6.1 (7.3)	31.0-33.0
East Germany	5.0	6.0 (6.9)	25.8-25.9
Soviet Union	4.7	6.3 (7.7)	28.0

SOURCE: Adapted from official documents released after adoption by Party Congresses in 1975.
*The figures in parentheses represent the average annual rate for the period 1971-1975.

The rate of growth is accelerated in the lagging national economies as reflected in a relatively higher rate of investment in the development plans. Although total investments will be maintained at a very high level, the figures for industrial growth show a somewhat lower projection in comparison with the previous five-year plan. In the case of the Soviet Union, the targets were slightly reduced because of the poor grain harvest of 1975, and similar reductions were made in Poland because of lagging agricultural production in 1976 (which contrasts with Poland's spectacular leap to tenth place among the industrial nations of the world).

I submit that under the historical conditions of the socialist societies, the development criterion will dominate internal and external policy. In forecasting the future one must keep in mind that unless the vital strategic goal of catching up with the developed capitalist nations is met, structural political changes could hardly occur in Eastern Europe. However, the picture will begin to change by 1990, when Eastern European nations plan to attain roughly the level of development prevailing in Western Europe. In such a totally new situation, the nations of Eastern Europe will then pass from the requirements of development to those of socialism. This will dictate a corresponding change in the political structure—whether smooth or disruptive is hard to predict. Surely, various international contingencies may accelerate or slow down the process.

Given the nature of global interdependencies, none of the three worlds functions in isolation. The industrial world and the socialist world are both parts of the world-system and as such are intersected by and interact with the other subsystems, whether East-South or North-South. The main theoretical point is that interdependence among systems or subsystems does not eliminate their autonomy. In the decentralized world of the 1980s the crosscutting tendencies will grow stronger in all international systems. The most consequential one to be envisaged is a rapprochement between China and Japan driven by the power game and by complementary economics. Such development would shift eastward the center of world politics.

THE YEAR 2000

As I read present historical trends, the world-system—with the nation-state as its fundamental structural unit, with the capitalist mode of production as its main organizational principle, and with the great powers acting as coordinate managers of world order—can no longer adhere to its old premises and is therefore under severe strain. Since the nation-state is the structural element of the system and hence the most enduring one, it is the mode of production and the role of the great powers that must undergo change in the next decades.

Thus, it is not accidental that the call for a new international order has been heard at this particular time and has instantly acquired worldwide appeal and urgency. Since its projection is likely to cover the remaining quarter of this century, which is also the period upon which modern social scientific projections focus, the new international order is bound to establish itself as the main axis of discussion in future studies on the year 2000.

The crises of the present international order are deep; their solution cannot be found in previous experience for they require worldwide participation and a global perspective. Therefore we must think anew and act anew. Radical changes inside societies have not solved contemporary problems. The call for a new international order is essentially a proposition to attack them from the other end—the world-system. But is this a practicable proposition?

As a Marxist, I should preface my answer by noting that what distinguishes my perspective from that of non-Marxist analysts is not only the theoretical model but also the role ascribed to revolutionary activity; that is, to the capability of men to interfere with history and influence its course according to a purpose. Hence, the Marxist perspective is probabilistic rather than deterministic: the basic assumption of this theory is not a single possible future but rather many possibilities out of which there will ultimately emerge, as a result of human intervention, only one. I.V. Bestujev-Lada is correct in opposing univocal prediction and in pleading for the study of factors that determine the most probable variant of producing a certain phenomenon or process among a certain scale of possibilities. Identifying the spectrum of possibilities and determining within this framework the distributive function of probabilities constitute the essence of projection of future social phenomena and processes.[21]

Let us hypothesize the various possible world political developments in a long-term perspective.

1. At the highest level of systemicity we can now perceive, we may anticipate three possibilities.

a. By the very fact that the call for a new international order came from the Group of 77 and that it involves primarily their relations with the developed nations, the North-South conflict will become central, which means that the national-strategic motive force will continue to be predominant in international politics. In this case, the chance of global war will be minimal although local military interventions and hostilities will still occur.

b. The alternative possibility may be realized if the economy of the developed world deteriorates to the point that the masses become so disenchanted with the capitalist system as to designate radical social change a must. Since such a situation would probably arise in a number of Western European nations, making it international in scope, social change would take on central significance and class-ideological motive force would again become paramount in world politics. This time, however, the polarization would not be limited to the East-West system, as in the years of the cold war. The old boundary—the iron curtain—no longer exists between West and East; rather, there are zones of interaction where inputs and outputs flow in and from outside, which would broaden the scope of the conflict.

In this case, a turbulent period would open up in world affairs that would involve great dangers of military adventurism and neofascism caused by the desperate attempts of finance and corporate capital to maintain its challenged position. Imperialism under intense pressure could precipitate a catastrophe whose proportions are hard to predict.

c. A third possible situation may arise if both the East-West and North-South conflicts reach a critical stage at the same time. In this case, the crosscutting and overlapping tendencies in the three worlds could result in the most fantastic coalitions ever conceived. Paradoxically, the chance of global war in such a chaotic situation would be smaller than in the preceding because the two converging conflicts would tend to cancel each other out.

2. Technological-interdependence pressure will increasingly produce regional unions of various forms and degrees of integration.

3. The beneficiaries of the world power structure will struggle against the creation of a new international order, resorting to dividing tactics, maneuvers, and ruses. Thus, power politics will follow nonideological lines, providing either an impetus to or a check on the process of integration.

4. National self-assertion in the developing continents will yield to social change. The privileged strata or social elites acting as the political agents of the capitalist metropoles will necessarily come into conflict with the forces of development and change.

5. A major result of the disintegration of the present world power structure will be the world institution.

The decentralization of power and the anarchy consequent upon the deterioration of the principle that keeps the world economy going, capitalism, will push to the fore the question of a world authority, as will transnational forces (particularly corporations).

The world of the next few decades will be a "small world" in which the per capita GNP of the developed nations will still be twelve times that of the developing ones even if the growth targets set by the United Nations are achieved. 22 The population ratio of the two groups of nations will be one to five. Anyone who puts these two sets of figures together must realize that the explosion will not be limited to population. We will live in a world in which it will take about two hours to fly from Buenos Aires to New York or from Lagos to London, a world in which the Bolivian or the Pakistani will see on television how people live in affluent societies, a world in which there will be no suburbia for the rich to insulate themselves from the poor. If present trends continue unchecked, the world of the year 2000 will live and sleep with a "balance of terror" in the hands of twenty or so ambitious nuclear nations, not to mention terrorist groups using atomic bombs for blackmail or ransom. Pollution will imperil the ecological balance, while problems of food, water, and weather may become critical. As the pillars of the old order crumble one after the other, the world of the year 2000 will look like New York, Tokyo, or Paris without traffic regulations and policemen to enforce them!

Surely, the United Nations is not equipped to deal with problems of such magnitude. A new type of international institution is required—a world institution with the authority to plan, make decisions, and enforce them.

This item is already on the agenda for it is organically linked with the establishment of a new international economic order. The Tinbergen Report rightly suggests a fundamental restructuring of the

United Nations so as to give it broad economic powers and a more decisive mandate for international economic decisionmaking. However, to be able to plan, make decisions, and enforce them, a world organization working on a truly democratic basis must be empowered by its members to do so. This report concludes that the achievement of such a global planning and management system calls for the conscious transfer of power—a gradual transfer to be sure—from the nation-state to the world organization. Only when this transfer has taken place can the organization become effective.[23]

Any agreement reached through north-south negotiations comes up against the issue of enforcement. Suppose, for the sake of argument, that an agreement linking prices of industrial goods with thos of raw materials is arrived at. How would it be enforced? Who will ensure that all the parties involved observe its provisions? The real choice is between a world authority and the laws of the market. And by now everybody knows that the laws of the market systematically work in favor of the rich industrial nations. Sooner or later, a world authority shall be established.

6. Finally, will the nation-state endure? Viewed as a model reduced to essentials, the nation-state has a double function: one directed inward—the instrument of class domination; the other directed outward—the armor of the nation against competition in the international arena. Most projections of the nation-state's future emphasize one function while neglecting the other. In the West those who argue that the state has become obsolete and should be abolished surely have not given much thought to the destiny of free enterprise in such a situation. Marx's emphasis was precisely the reverse, neglecting the international function of the state. In fact, it is hard to say which of the two types of society needs the state most at the present time. To the developing nations the state is equally indispensable not only as the molder of the nation but also as the best weapon in the battle for development.

Marx's anticipation of the withering away of the state was postulated for the final stage of the communist society, a stage that is further from the socialist stage than socialist society is from capitalist. Without entering into a theoretical debate on this thesis, one point now seems clear: such a phenomenon cannot be viewed exclusively in terms of the internal development of society. If internal conditions are decisive in making a revolution and building "socialism in one country," then international conditions are decisive in establishing a communist society. To begin with, a civilization superior to the capitalist one may take shape only when the economic and social parameters of the latter have been transcended. Moreover, it is inconceivable that a nation would renounce its state power as long as discrepancies in size, military strength, and wealth among nations give rise to rivalries and conflicts. The communist civilization is conceivable only in a world-system in which present inequalities and patterns of behavior have been eliminated.

CONCLUSION

In a long-term perspective, the dissolution of national power must be projected in the context of both the process of international integration and the establishment of a strong world institution. Ideally, the two processes should advance gradually and in parallel, thus ensuring an orderly transfer of power from the nation to the forms of higher systemicity: the regional communities, followed by continental groupings and the world authority. However, one must view these historical processes in the perspective of the dual and contradictory motion that is at work in world politics. The dialectical interaction between the two is likely to extend well into the next century, when global integration may be in sight.

As mentioned in the Preface, the remaining two decades of this century may go down in history as its most critical and explosive period. Therefore, the overriding challenge of this period of painful transition may not be the control of population, energy, pollution, or weather, but the control of power.

NOTES

1. Lewis S. Feuer, ed., *Marx and Engels* (New York: Doubleday, Anchor, 1959), p. 5.
2. Herman Kahn and Anthony Wiener, *The Year 2000* (New York: Macmillan, 1967).
3. Ibid., p. 187.
4. Ibid.
5. Zbigniew Brzezinski, *Between Two Ages* (New York: Viking Press, 1970).
6. Ibid., p. 296.
7. Radovan Richta, ed., *Civilizatia la rascruce* [Civilization at the crossroads] (Bucharest: Ed. Politica, 1970).
8. Ibid., pp. 56-63.
9. Richard A. Falk, *A Study of Future Worlds* (New York: Free Press, 1975).
10. Alexandre Faire and Jean-Paul Sebord, *Le nouveau déséquilibre mondial* (Paris: Grasset, 1973).

11. Ibid., Introduction.

12. Ibid., p. 11.

13. Ibid., p. 15.

14. James N. Rosenau, Kenneth Thompson, and Gavin Boyd, eds., *World Politics* (New York: Free Press, 1976).

15. Mihajlo Mesarovic and Eduard Pestel, *Stratégie pour demain* (Paris: Seuil, 1974).

16. Wassily Leontief, ed., *The Future of the World Economy* (New York: United Nations, 1976).

17. Zbigniew Brzezinski, "Specter of an Isolated America in a Hostile World," *International Herald Tribune*, 3 January 1977.

18. Silviu Brucan, "A Romanian Looks at Italian Communists," *New York Times*, 2 July 1976.

19. "Nyerere: Socialism a Long Way Off," *International Herald Tribune*, 21 April 1977.

20. "Arab Plan to Turn Sudan into Region's Breadbasket," *International Herald Tribune*, 3 February 1977.

21. I. V. Bestujev-Lada, *Okno v buduscee* [Window to the future] (Moscow: Misl, 1970).

22. Leontief, ed., op. cit.

23. Jan Tinbergen, coordinator, *Reshaping the International Order* (New York: Dutton, 1976), p. 185.

Index

Adler-Karlsson, Gunnar, 103
Aggregation, 18–20
Agriculture, 6, 19, 38
Alaska, 85
Albania, 52, 54, 103, 104
Alger, Chadwick, 134
Algeria, 73, 81, 125
Amin, Samir, 57
Angola, 24, 71, 147
Anticommunism, 7
Arab Authority, 148
Arab League, 123
Aron, Raymond, 25
Aryan superiority, 4
Ascent of Man, The (Bronowski), 140*n*.
Athens, 71
Atomic strategy, crisis of, 46
Austria, 22, 90
Autonomy, 18–20, 150

Balance of power, 58–59, 71
Balance of terror, 122, 152
Balancing on the brink-of-war policy, 117, 122
Ball, George, 115
Base and superstructure, theory of, 9–10, 11, 48
Behaviorism, 3
Belgium, 81, 88, 89, 130, 133
Bell, Daniel, 25, 81–82
Benelux arrangement, 95
Berlin, 72
Berlinguer, Enrico, 63
Bestujev-Lada, I. V., 151
Between Two Ages (Brzezinski), 139
Bio-organic school, 4–5
Bipolarity, 59, 62, 72, 75, 115, 125
Bismarck, Otto von, 94
Blair, John, 131
Bodin, Jean, 2
Bohemia, 90
Bolivia, 24
Boulding, Kenneth, 116, 117, 122
Bourgeois, Emile, 1
Bourgeoisie, 15, 21, 53
Brazil, 25, 86, 147
Brest-Litovsk, Peace of, 17, 27
Bretton Woods conference, 125

British Commonwealth, 87, 95
Bronowski, Jacob, 140*n*.
Brzezinski, Zbigniew, 8, 76, 139, 145
Bucharin, Nikolai, 42
Bulgaria, 103, 105–107, 149

Caesar, Julius, 44
Calculated risk, 122
Cambodia, 63, 147
Canada, 81, 131, 145
Capital investment, 69
Capitalism, 1, 6, 7, 37, 40*n*., 42, 49, 52–58, 67, 70, 108, 152
Carrillo, Santiago, 63
Chace, James, 11
Chamberlain, H. S., 4
Chamberlain, Neville, 42
Chile, 133, 146
China, 19, 35, 36, 42, 54, 109, 148, 150
    power structure, 59, 63
    Soviet Union, relations with, 23, 51, 95, 103, 120, 147
    United Nations and, 115
    U.S., relations with, 63
Chou En-lai, 148
Churchill, Sir Winston, 42
City-states, 20, 71
Civilization at the Crossroads (ed. Richta), 140
Class
    conflict, 3, 16, 21–24, 81–83
    foreign policy formation and, 38–40
    ideology, 24–27
    integration and, 86–88
    national motivation and, 21–24
    in primitive societies, 18–20
    ruling, 20, 42–43, 45, 87, 140
    state system and leadership and, 41–45
Coercive power, 96
Cold war, 23–25, 36, 103, 115, 117, 122
Colombia, 24
Colonialism, 17, 37, 57
COMECON: *see* Council for Mutual Economic Assistance (CMEA)
Comintern, 95